SMUGGLING IN CORNWALL

An Illustrated History

Jeremy Rowett Johns

AMBERLEY

First published 2016

Amberley Publishing
The Hill, Stroud,
Gloucestershire, GL5 4EP

www.amberley-books.com

ISBN: 978 1 4456 5168 2 (print)
ISBN: 978 1 4456 5169 9 (ebook)

British Library Cataloguing in Publication Data.
A catalogue record for this book is available from the British Library.

Typeset in 10pt on 13pt Celeste.
Typesetting by Amberley Publishing.
Printed in the UK.

Contents

Introduction

Running a contraband cargo by moonlight into a picturesque cove lit by beacons on the cliffs may be a romanticised view of Cornish smuggling. There were occasionally fierce and bloody clashes between the smugglers and Revenue men, and even murder was not unknown; it could be a brutal business and the traffic in cheap spirits encouraged an even greater degree of drunkenness among the population.

Depriving the government of revenue extorted by high taxes was regarded by most Cornish folk as a legitimate activity; magistrates turned a blind eye, juries refused to convict, short-sighted Excise men accepted tubs of brandy as bribes and the law against smugglers was far less ferocious than that against thieves. By 1770, some 470,000 gallons of brandy and 350,000 pounds of tea were being smuggled into Cornwall every year at a cost of about £150,000 to the Exchequer.

The Napoleonic wars at the end of the eighteenth century had a particularly bad effect on the fishing industry, not only by the loss of overseas markets but also by the heavy duties that were levied on salt, which was essential for curing pilchards. Fishermen were often unable to earn enough to buy salt to preserve sufficient pilchards for their own families and sometimes the fish were simply left to provide manure for the farmers. On at least one occasion, when the St Ives fishermen had a great haul of pilchards in their nets, they left them in shallow water until salt had been smuggled from France to cure them. Small wonder, therefore, that smuggling became a major industry in Cornwall during the hard times of the French wars.

AN ENGLISH SMUGGLER.

An English smuggler. (© National Maritime Museum, London)

An innocent catch of pilchards being landed, or contraband being brought ashore?

Seventeenth Century

It is likely that Customs officers were stationed at Cornish ports active in seaborne trade as early as the Middle Ages.

Up to the middle of the eighteenth century, port frauds appear to have been more prevalent than illegal landings. Customs officers were often bribed to turn a blind eye to the import of dutiable goods, or to underweigh them. As the service became more professional, there was less opportunity for such dishonesty, and the smuggling industry grew up. The coves and bays of Cornwall were ideally suited for illegal landings of spirits, wine and tea from France; all these were high duty items, and for periods of several years at a time their import was prohibited altogether because of war or trade rivalry.

The collection of the Customs in each principal port of England was administered by three Crown officers appointed by letters patent – the customer, the controller and the searcher – an arrangement that had existed from medieval times.

The system of port books – one kept by each Customs officer – had operated from 1565, being sent to the Exchequer by the officers in the regional head ports, which in the case of Cornwall were Plymouth, Looe, Fowey, Truro, Falmouth, Penryn, Gweek, Penzance, the Scillies, St Ives and Padstow.

Goods seized by the officers as contraband were reported to London, and the Commissioners then decided whether to prosecute. They were then proclaimed in the court in Westminster Hall, and if not claimed would be condemned and disposed of, bids being invited; if a purchaser was found, the goods were released to him. If a claim was made the case would be tried with a jury. If no bids were forthcoming and the goods remained unclaimed, they were awarded to the seizing officer if he was prepared to pay the value.

Such a blanket prohibition invited fraud and, if that failed, then actual smuggling. Widespread Customs frauds all through the south-western ports led the Customs commissioners to send an experienced official, William Culliford, on a tour of inquiry. He visited Looe in 1683 and his report covering Looe and neighbouring ports, signed at Plymouth, was presented to the Treasury the following year. It is full of fascinating detail, and provides evidence of smuggling locally at a period when such evidence is hard to come by.

Port frauds seem to have been particularly prevalent up to the middle of the eighteenth century, but as the Customs service was gradually made more professional and less corrupt, port frauds became less frequent and illegal landings became more important to the smugglers. Certainly this was the case in the port of Looe, though 'less corrupt' must be taken to exclude matters of political patronage.

Looe was an insignificant port compared to Plymouth, but was near enough to participate in smuggling from ships trading with its larger neighbour. In addition, most Looe ships, as Culliford found when he investigated the other Cornish ports, constantly smuggled goods into Polperro and were also engaged in the illicit export of Cornish tin.

Few of the Looe officers escaped Culliford's criticism. The Customs collector, Philip Stephens, was clearly corrupt and appears to have had a finger in most of the fraud that occurred there at the time. So much so that he was the only Looe officer who Culliford brought charges against. Stephens habitually refrained from destroying large quantities of seized contraband and regularly omitted to search Looe and Plymouth ships coming from overseas carrying only cargoes of salt. When he did catch smugglers in the act, or came across smuggled goods in merchants' premises, he would extract a bribe rather than seize the goods. Stephens was too corrupt to survive and Culliford suspended him on the spot.

At the time of Culliford's visit to Cornwall, the seagoing commerce of the Cornish ports was modest compared with that of many West Country ports. Maritime activity was dominated by fishing and the coastal trade, the latter consisting mainly of the export of tin and copper and the import of wine, tobacco, iron, coal, cider, corn and miscellaneous wares

East and West Looe.

West Looe.

from other English ports. But Cornwall had a tradition of smuggling and many Cornish merchants were engaged in illegal activity, while the native population at all levels was particularly reluctant to the payment of customs and other duties.

In 1682, for example, Hugh Jones, a magistrate near Land's End, not only stored his own smuggled wine in his house but also that of his neighbours, and refused access to Customs men to search his premises. Another prominent merchant investigated by Culliford was James Kemp of Penryn, known to be heavily involved with dishonest Customs officers. Kemp was Mayor of Penryn and a powerful local figure whose highly organised, large-scale and persistent smuggling had gone unchallenged. He had specially constructed hiding places to store his smuggled goods from abroad, mainly prohibited French silks, hats, linen, wine and brandy. These included a secret storeroom in his house, accessible through a cupboard in the bedroom, and another – reached through a trapdoor under a bed – which was large enough to take the whole cargo of a small ship.

As a result of William Culliford's tour of the Cornish ports, some nineteen senior Customs officers were dismissed, suspended or allowed to resign; others, though guilty of misconduct, were demoted or moved elsewhere. Despite all this, Cornish smuggling was not eliminated. Merchants continued to perpetrate tobacco and other frauds and Customs officers continued to be dismissed for corruption.

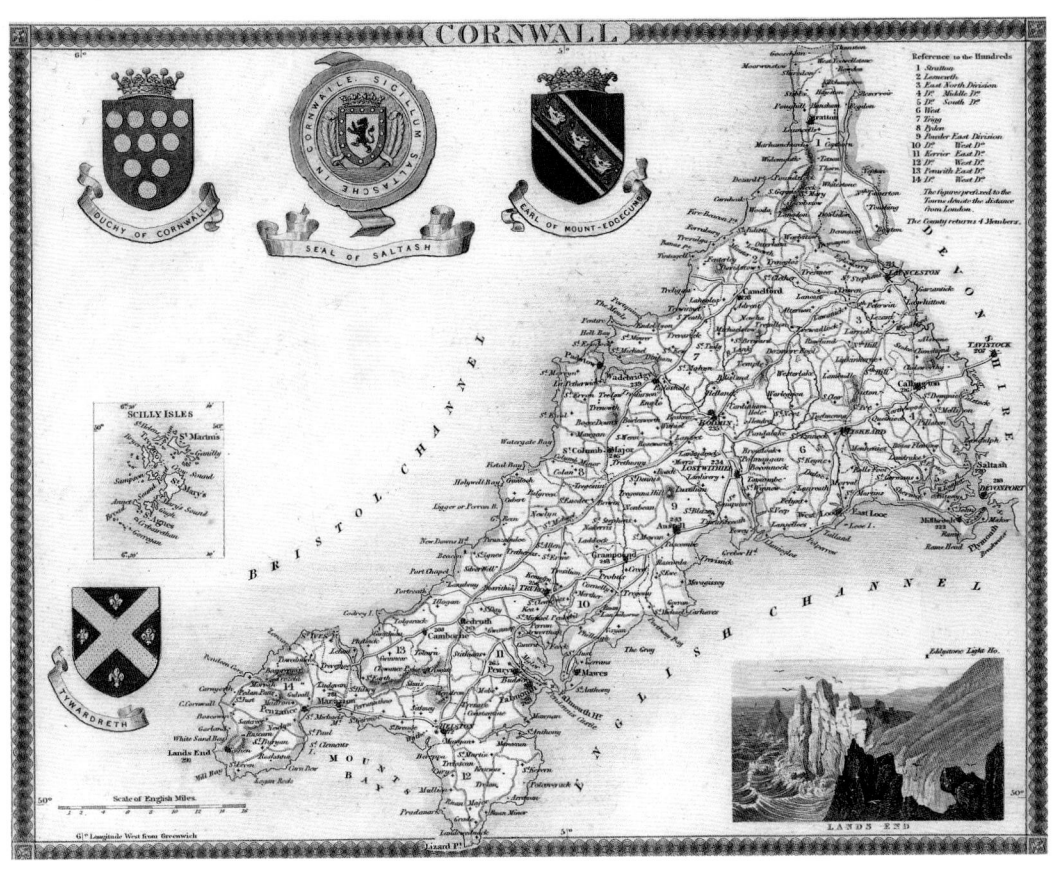

1836 map of Cornwall by Thomas Moule.

Opposite above: A run of goods.

Opposite below: The Lizard from Kynance Cove.

A SHIP HAS BEEN SIGHTED

in this quarter

ENGAGING IN THE UNLAWFUL ACT OF

SMUGGLING

whosoever can lay information
leading to the capture of this ship
or its crew

will receive a reward of

£500

From His Majesty's Government

This 19th day of October 1782

Smuggling poster.

Eighteenth Century

In general, in the eighteenth century the only people authorised by the Board of Customs apart from its own employees were Excise and Salt Tax officers, naval officers, extra tide waiters and boatmen. Soldiers were directed to assist Customs operations, though apparently only to aid those holding commission. Boats, horses and carriages used to convey smuggled goods were made subject to seizure, in addition to the contraband itself. If goods were stopped on suspicion or information, they were taken to the Customs warehouse.

Higher duties and higher prices because of the recurring French wars made the eighteenth century the heyday of the smugglers of south Cornwall. Through their connections with Brittany and Guernsey they maintained a constant supply of liquor, wine, tea and tobacco, to name only the mainstays of their trade. Successive British governments had imposed high duties on a variety of luxury goods imported from Europe, initially to protect trade with the North American colonies, and smuggling became exceptionally profitable for anyone prepared to face little more risk than most people encountered in their everyday struggle to earn a livelihood. Understaffed Revenue authorities were invariably powerless to prevent the smugglers, who were often protected by a sympathetic public.

Brandy, gin, tea and tobacco were all readily available across the Channel at considerably lower prices than they were in England, where such commodities attracted heavy duties and were often unobtainable. By 1770, some 469,000 gallons of brandy and 350,000 pounds of tea alone were being smuggled into Cornwall every year, amounting to the considerable loss of some £150,000 to the Exchequer.

As the Channel Islands were exempt from any taxation imposed by a British parliament, they become the main centre for the supply of contraband goods into Britain during the seventeenth and eighteenth centuries. The Guernsey merchants at St Peter Port imported large quantities of geneva (gin) from Rotterdam, brandy from France and Spain, rum from the West Indies, tobacco from Virginia and tea via the powerful East India Company from China. Most of these commodities were sold on to English wholesalers and smugglers.

Cornwall's proximity to Guernsey ensured such trade was particularly active there, but the 100 miles or more of sea separating it from St Peter Port involved a hazardous voyage for small fishing vessels in all but the most favourable weather, even in times of peace. With only the crudest of navigational instruments to guide them, the men who made the perilous crossing often risked death at sea and many were lost in the attempt to bring back contraband goods.

When the tax on salt was increased by the young William Pitt in order to raise money to pay for the wars against France, Cornish pilchard fishing communities were particularly hard hit. Large quantities of salt were used in preserving pilchards for markets both at home and abroad, and the extra tax burden only served to encourage an illegitimate trade with Britain's enemy, France, from which much salt was normally obtained. For ordinary folk, the only way to get cheap salt to cure enough fish for their own families was by smuggling it into the country. It required a bushel of salt to cure a thousand pilchards, barely enough to supply a moderately large family throughout the winter, but the duty on such a quantity of English salt, amounting to 3s 4d (6s 8d for foreign salt), represented nearly half the wages made in a poor fishing season.

Britain's restrictive trading laws and high taxes also led to her North American colonies making their historic Declaration of Independence in 1776. When war broke out between Britain and the rebel colonists, France and Spain joined the rebels in order to gain revenge on Britain for territorial and trade losses suffered in earlier years.

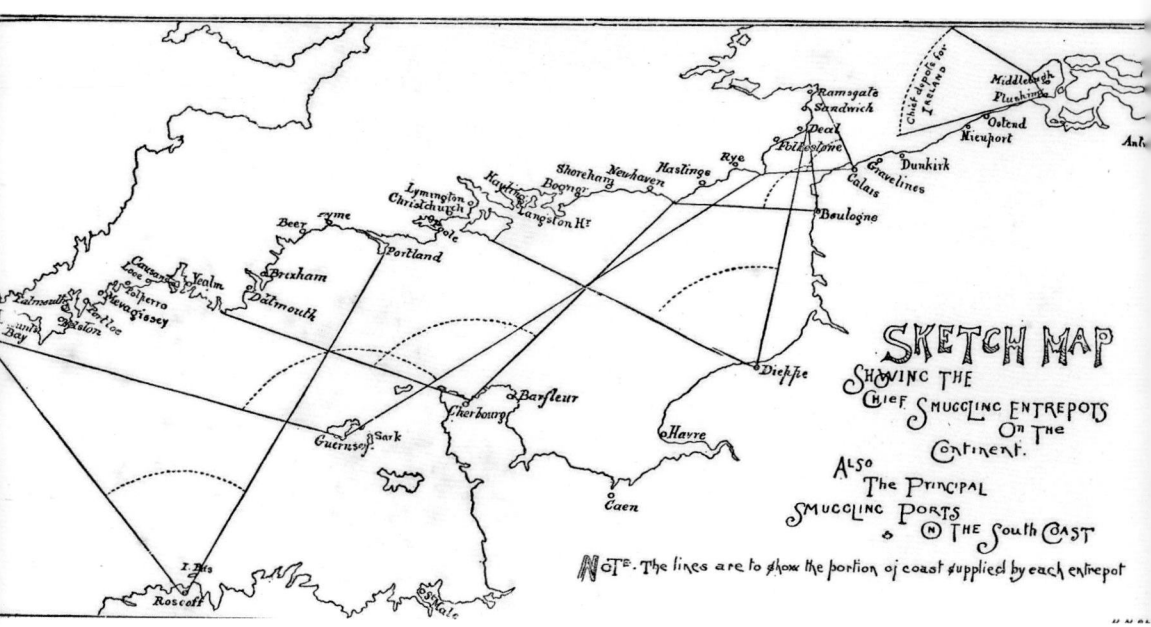

Sketch map.

Boats

Smugglers required small, light but sturdy vessels capable of carrying a large amount of sail. They had to be able to beach anywhere and be capable of carrying between 400 and 800 ankers (10-gallon casks) of spirits. Another requirement was for small rowing boats that could pick up cargoes that had been sunk offshore.

A high proportion of the vessels registered at ports along the south coast of Cornwall in the eighteenth century were engaged in smuggling. Many were built specially for the purpose at shipbuilding yards, such as those at Mevagissey where the vagaries of the pilchard fishery particularly encouraged illegal trading. The high import tariffs, raised again and again to pay for the wars with France and Spain, made the profits from smuggling very tempting indeed.

The nearby port of Fowey was also another notorious smugglers' resort, one of several places around the coast where Customs sloops had been established. Many of the vessels registered there during the 1790s were either sloops or cutters of clinker construction; fast, handy and manoeuvrable.

In an attempt to curb the 'trade', as it was known, complex regulations were imposed upon the design and rigs that could give smuggling vessels advantage in speed and manoeuvrability. An anti-smuggling Act in 1779, for example, made ships of under 200 tons carrying goods in illegal packages subject to forfeit, and boats with more than four oars were forbidden. But anti-smuggling legislation in the eighteenth and early nineteenth centuries failed to achieve its purpose, largely because it coincided with other legislation that raised duties and therefore the potential profits to be made from smuggling.

During the Napoleonic wars, many boats were converted into privateers and launched complete with twelve to sixteen gun ports and deck stanchions. The sail area was often increased by fitting a longer bowsprit in order to give the extra turn of speed necessary for privateering. This was all very well as long as the vessel was engaged in legitimate cruising against the enemy, but if and when she indulged in a little smuggling and was chased, she could easily outstrip the slower Revenue cutter. Hence the official precautions taken to ensure that such luggers should, unless actually in commission as privateers, be fitted with shorter 'legal' bowsprits.

It was not unusual for these vessels to be impounded, as in March 1791 when the Customs Board in London informed the Plymouth officials:

A vessel between 60 and 70 feet long, lately built at Mevagissey for the smuggling employ, and owned by John Quiller of Polperro, has sailed from Mevagissey without being registered. She was then rigged as a sloop, but it is supposed she has since altered into a lugger...

A month later, they wrote again:

Having read your reports in return to our enquiry on the petition of John Quiller praying the delivery of a vessel called the Betsy under seizure at your port, on account of the bowsprit exceeding the dimensions prescribed by law, we have rejected his request and direct you to prosecute the vessel in the Exchequer.

The *Betsy* would have suffered the usual fate of vessels condemned under the increasingly stringent anti-smuggling laws and, unless taken into service by the revenue service, would have been sawn through in three places to ensure that she never put to sea again. Regulations were introduced affecting the construction, equipment and crewing of sailing craft. Any vessel of more than 50 tons rigged as a lugger or having a bowsprit more than two thirds its own length was liable to forfeiture. The law struck at everything concerned with smuggling. Boats, horses and carts used in the landing or transporting of contraband goods were seized and sold. The mere fact of loitering near the coast was sufficient to bring someone, however innocent their intentions, within the law's grasp:

Boys with boat in harbour.

Any person loitering within five miles of the sea-coast or any navigable river, with intent, as is suspected, to assist in running goods, is to be brought before a justice; and if unable to give a satisfactory account of his calling or employment, shall be committed to the House of Correction, to be whipped and kept to hard labour for any time not exceeding one month.

The threat of such harsh penalties did little to deter the smugglers, however. When the young William Pitt reduced some of the heaviest duties on imports soon after he became prime minister in 1784 in the hope of discouraging the activities of smugglers, the trade between Guernsey and Cornwall continued unabated. In the same year, a new Hovering Act was introduced. Various types of clinker-built vessels commonly used, or even specially built, for smuggling were now required to be licensed, their owner giving security that they would not in fact be used in the smuggling trade. Unlicensed vessels of the types specified were liable to be seized, with their cargoes, if found within 4 leagues of the coast.

Sinking stones were attached and kept on deck until just before slipping the cargo.

Left: Mevagissey harbour, 1909.

Below: St Peter Port, Guernsey, 1790s. Watercolour by Joshua Gosselin.

The Guernsey Merchants

The Cornish smugglers obtained the bulk of their supplies from Guernsey. The merchants there imported wines and spirits and stored them in their vaults and caves, ideal for maturing purposes; they bought in bulk and shipped out in smaller casks to any customers who could pay – many of them smugglers from Cornwall. So great was the trade that a secondary industry grew up around it: the manufacture of casks – small, easily carried kegs of 10 gallons known as ankers. By the time British anti-smuggling legislation had been extended to the Channel Islands in 1805, and a Custom House set up in St Peter Port, there were at least 600 coopers engaged in making them. The vaults and stores in the town were overflowing and some cargoes were even hidden under temporary coverings in the surrounding fields above.

The bustling town and harbour of St Peter Port was the key to Guernsey's prosperity during the latter half of the eighteenth century. Its freedom from import duties, deep anchorage sheltered by the neighbouring islands and entrance guarded by the heavily fortified Castle Cornet made it the best haven in the Channel Islands. It was here during the wars between Britain and France that the Guernsey merchants grew rich on the profits of privateering and the smuggling trade with England.

Exempt from taxation imposed by Parliament, it became the single most important centre for the supply of a wide range of contraband goods into Britain during the eighteenth and nineteenth centuries. The annual revenue from smuggling, or 'free trade' as the islanders preferred to call it, exceeded £40,000 at its height, more than the total value of Guernsey's legitimate exports to England in the course of a year. Guernsey traders at St Peter Port imported large quantities of wines and spirits, almost all for sale to English wholesalers and smugglers. The wine and brandy stored in vaults in the town matured very well in Guernsey's mild climate and this, together with the island's strategic position between France and Britain, combined to make it one of the chief entrepôts of smuggling.

It was thanks to privateering and smuggling, together with shipbuilding and coopering, that some island families made great fortunes, while many others enjoyed considerable wealth for the first time.

A group of Guernsey merchants based in London played an important part in the business and financial affairs of the island companies involved in exporting to England,

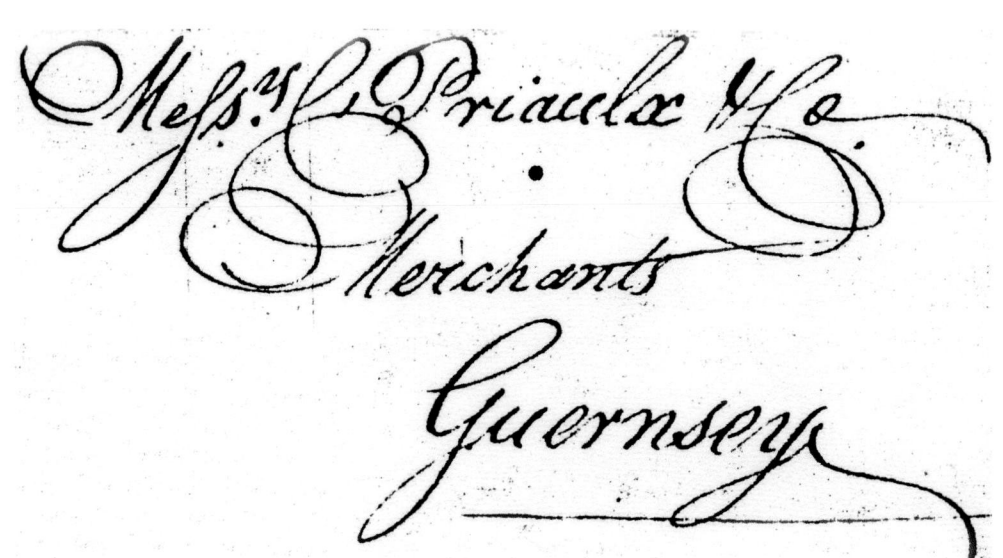

Messrs Carteret Priaulx & Co. – merchants from Guernsey.

including the supplying of smugglers, and in the latter part of the century the setting out and management of privateers. One of them, Thomas Priaulx (1725–1784), became a junior partner in the firm of Carteret de Jersey at some time in the 1750s, and the accounts of that firm for 1766 and 1767 show him actively engaged in the business of supplying spirits and tea to outlets in Cornwall. In the 1760s the agent who covered Cornwall for the firm then known as Carteret Jersey & Co. was Joseph Edyvean of St Austell. The Guernsey merchants allowed their Cornish customers considerable credit. They visited the mainland from time to time, but their agent Edyvean and his successors spent much of their time in debt collecting as well as arranging purchases. Eventually, in 1808, an Act of Parliament brought the Channel Islands within the British Customs net. Much, but not all, of the trade in supplying smugglers went to France, notably Roscoff in Brittany.

By the 1780s Edyvean's place seems to have been taken by Charles Guy, who kept the Ship Inn at Polperro and was a man of business almost rivalling Zephaniah Job himself, with whom he was contemporary. While no actual correspondence of Edyvean appears to have survived in the Carteret Priaulx papers, there are many letters from Guy, who collected and transmitted multiple orders from Polperro smugglers for tea and liquor.

From time to time the Guernsey merchants would come across from the island in person, calling on their agents such as Job and Charles Guy and chasing up outstanding debts. On one such visit in April 1805, Carteret Priaulx was in Cornwall checking accounts and collecting debts. Arriving in Polperro, he called on Charles Guy at the Ship Inn, only to find the family mourning the death of Guy's brother-in-law, William Rowett, the previous night. 'Excess of drink has killed him,' he told his brothers in Guernsey.

The prospect that Parliament might soon end smuggling from Guernsey did not seem to worry Carteret very much. 'I am glad we shall not be long troubled with this damn business,' he wrote, and later the same month, while in Cornwall, he expressed hopes that if just two or three more smuggling voyages could be made, they would reduce the firm's

Right: Reginald Puckey, one of many Polperro fishermen photographed by Lewis Harding in the 1860s. Could he have been one of the smugglers?

Below left: A tranquil enough scene in Looe harbour in the last century, but beneath the surface a flourishing trade in smuggled goods from Guernsey continued, often under the noses of the Revenue officers.

Below right: Polperro's narrow streets were the scene of many a confrontation between the smugglers and Revenue men in the 1790s.

stock before the British anti-smuggling Acts were applied for the first time to Guernsey and end the trade.

By the summer of 1805 the traffic of smuggled goods from Guernsey to Cornwall was at a low ebb, due in part to the vigilance of the Revenue cruisers patrolling the Channel during the long hours of daylight, but also because the threat of new anti-smuggling laws deterred venturers.

SHIP INN,
POLPERRO,
KEPT BY
CHARLES GUY.

Trewman and Haydon, Printers, Plymouth.

Eating			
Wine			
Negus			
Rum			
Brandy			
Geneva			
Punch	0	1	3
Toddy			
Shrub			
Flip			
Beer			
Cyder	0	0	2
Cherry Brandy			
Rafpberry ditto			
Coffee			
Tea	0	2	8
Firing			
Tobacco	0	2	0
Lodging			
Servants Eating			
Drinking			
Hay	0	2	8
Corn	0	2	0
Smith			
Oftler			
Chambermaid			
Waiter			
Boots			
	0	10	9
Servants	0	2	0
	0	12	9

Mess.rs C [illegible] & Co

Gen.tn You will please to ship onboard of the Sedwell on Acct. of Richd Clements 20 Ankers Gin 18 Brandy & 2 Rum this day he has Paid me £20. on Acct of Sisters lost bill.

am Gen.tn Your humble servt.

Polperro April 13. 1798. Chas Guy

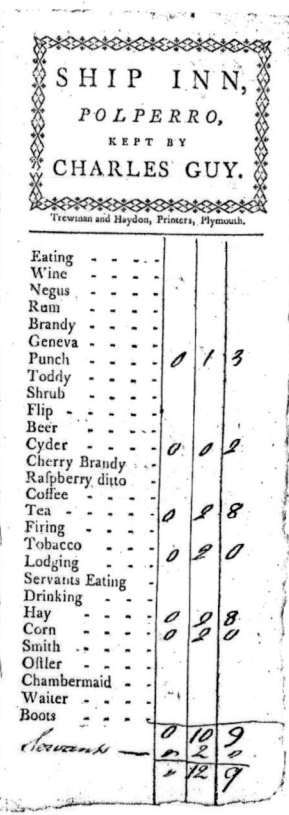

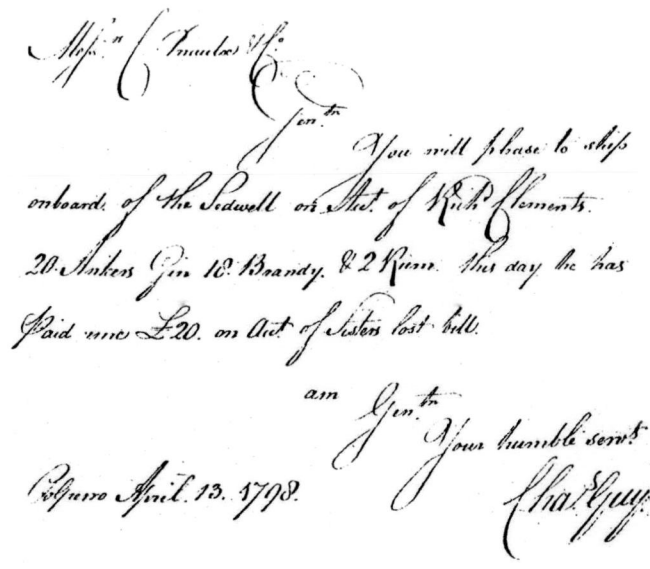

Above: Letter to Guernsey merchants dated 13 April 1798 from Charles Guy, landlord of the Ship Inn in Polperro, asking them to 'ship on board the *Sedwell* on Acct. of Richard Clements 20 ankers of gin, 18 brandy & 2 rum'.

Left: Ship Inn, Polperro, kept by Charles Guy.

Below: Packhorses with cargo.

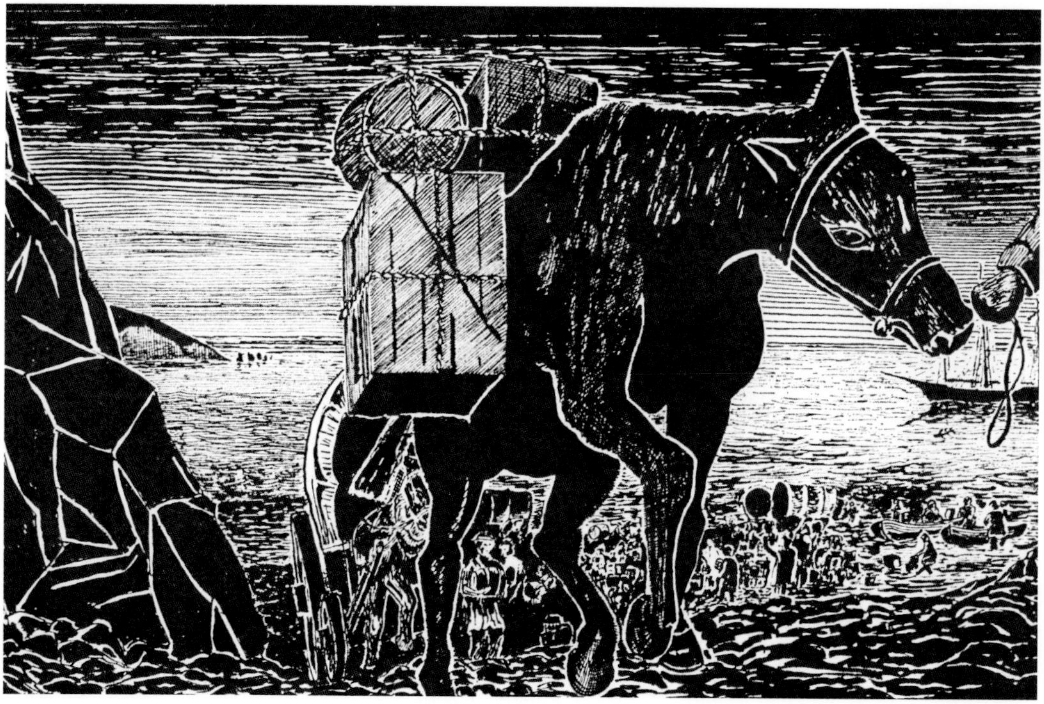

The Revenue Men

Just after daybreak on Ash Wednesday in March 1794, a formidable party came tramping through the narrow streets of the little fishing village of Polperro in south Cornwall. It consisted of four Excise men – the supervisor at Bodmin, and officers of Bodmin, Fowey and Lostwithiel – escorted by fourteen soldiers of the Yorkshire Militia. They made their way to the house of Thomas Pinsent, the resident Customs officer at Polperro.

The Revenue men had received a tip that if they raided certain houses in the village they would find substantial quantities of spirits, stored after being run and awaiting distribution. They required Pinsent to come with them, no doubt because of his local knowledge, as well as the fact that he was supposedly responsible for the district. Just because he had to live in Polperro, he may have regarded the summons to help raid his neighbours' houses with some trepidation.

Warrants had been prepared the evening before, and the party including Pinsent set off. They first went to the house of a man named Bennett, which Pinsent pointed out as worth searching. All they found was a 5-gallon tub in the back yard. They went on down the street to the house of Richard Rowett, which they recognised because it was opposite a lime kiln. The door was shut, and knocking produced no answer. It was a house like others that can be seen today near Polperro harbour, with the front door at the head of a flight of steps, living quarters on the first floor and a cellar beneath. Just then Rowett came along the street and mounted the steps, where David Llewyn, the Excise supervisor, stood outside the door. Llewyn read the search warrant to Rowett, who in turn knocked on the door, but no one opened up.

About the middle of the stairs was a little window that opened into the cellar, which was covered with a kind of shutter. Llewyn kicked the shutter, which gave way; a soldier was sent in through the window and unlocked the door. Inside was an Aladdin's cave – some 200 or 300 casks of liquor. The raiding party bored into one with a gimlet and tasted the contents. It proved to be brandy, so they seized the lot in the king's name and asked Pinsent if they could deposit them in his house. He agreed, and sixteen tubs, containing 65 gallons of brandy and 15 of Geneva, were carried to Pinsent's house – 'Tubs' was the local name for the casks; they were small barrels, slung about with cords so that the smugglers could transport them overland. Then the party heard an outbreak of gunfire, coming from the direction of the quay, some 200 yards from Rowett's cellar.

There appeared to be several guns on swivels, and soon there was a hostile crowd of over 100 people, some of them armed with guns and clubs or big sticks. The angry crowd stopped the soldiers, who were heavily outnumbered, from carrying away any more of the tubs. Someone shut the door, saying that anyone who tried to continue the seizure would be murdered. The fourteen soldiers were drawn up, with their muskets. Pinsent, who knew his Polperro neighbours, appealed to Llewyn 'for God's sake not to let the soldiers fire ... for if you do we shall all be murdered.' Llewyn told the crowd that he was not there to molest them, and invited them to let him take the goods out of the town. They said they would be damned if he should, and they would defend their property with their lives if necessary.

Three swivel-guns were pointed towards the cellar door through which the officers would have to pass to remove the rest of the tubs. One of the Excise officers ordered five or six soldiers to fix their bayonets. Eight or ten of the crowd were armed with guns, and in the narrow street came up close to the Revenue men, who had no room to manoeuvre. With the mob was John Langmaid who had a bayonet in one hand and a fusee – a type of gun – in the other. He threatened to run Llewyn through if he did not desist.

Meanwhile, someone had set up a swivel gun in the street, elevated and pointing at the raiding party. One officer saw three more guns behind it. Llewyn at last decided his life was in danger and retired, presently accompanied by his colleagues and the soldiers, to a local inn where they called for a legitimate drink or two to fortify themselves, and settled down to wait. After half an hour Llewyn asked Pinsent, the local man, to go down and see whether the crowd had calmed down and were more inclined to surrender the smuggled goods. When he came back Pinsent reported that it was of no use, the men would not yield.

The forces of law and order decided that discretion was the better part, and retreated, only to return several weeks later with a force of over 100 soldiers to arrest three men, not for smuggling, but for armed opposition to David Llewyn, the Excise supervisor. This detachment filed down the narrow Polperro streets only to find that, not surprisingly, the birds had flown. In the end only one of them – John Langmaid – was found and arrested. To avoid either local violence or a partisan jury, he was taken to London and tried at the Old Bailey the following year. The evidence against Langmaid was overwhelming, and he was the only one of the accused who was available for the authorities to make an example. The jury found him guilty, and he was sentenced to death.

That, however, was not the end of the matter. The authorities had reckoned without Zephaniah Job, who looked after his own and had influence in high places. With the help of several influential members of the Cornish gentry he persuaded the High Sheriff, R. A. Daniell, to write 'a strong letter' to the Home Secretary, the Duke of Portland, to secure a reprieve. The efforts succeeded and a royal pardon was granted to Langmead, subject to his serving in the Navy.

Sometimes the Customs men put forward a case which was not felt worth prosecuting, but which perhaps they felt was necessary to propose in order to justify themselves. In 1798 there were no fewer than three Riding officers attached to the port of Looe; how far this was due to patronage and how far to the increase of smuggling is hard to say. Their areas overlapped, and one of the three – Nathaniel Hearle – was assigned to the stretch of coast from Crafthole to Polperro. In March that year he swore a King's Bench affidavit against a Polperro publican for aiding smugglers. Hearle described his own status as 'gentleman', something few Customs officers would have felt themselves justified in doing. Aged about forty-five, he was a prominent burgess of West Looe and later that year was to become mayor of the borough, as he had been on several previous occasions. On the afternoon of 24 January 1798, Hearle stated, he was on his ride when he fell in with a party of smugglers in a lane near Crumplehorn, where the mill is still a tourist site. The men were loading their horses with kegs, in the way smugglers usually carried their goods; the first horse that Hearle came up with had four kegs on it, and others were lying in the road.

Hearle told a man who was standing by, whose name he did not know, that he was a Customs officer, then took his gimlet to bore a hole in one of the kegs to check its contents. Before he could do this a man named Charles Hoyton, who kept a public house in Polperro and was a reputed smuggler, seeing that no one came to Hearle's assistance called out to the men `Drive on – there is no danger.' The men picked up the kegs that were on the ground, drove on their horses, and told Hearle to keep off. He followed them for ¼ mile, during which time they threatened him with the clubs they were carrying, bragging that even if there were five Customs officers present they would not be taken. Nathaniel Hearle decided that discretion was the better part 'and judging his life would be in danger if he should follow them any farther with much disappointment and regret gave up the pursuit.' He added, and this must have ruined his case, that the publican Hoyton did not go on with the party after urging them to drive on, nor did he know whether any of the kegs belonged to Hoyton, and that he only assisted the smugglers as he had described.

CUSTOM-HOUSE, LONDON,
14th December, 1814.

WHEREAS it has been represented to the Commissioners of His Majesty's Customs, that on the night of the 7th instant, John Smith, Commander of the HIND cutter, in the service of the Customs, and his crew, when about to take possession of a Smuggling Vessel in the Harbour of Mevagissey, in the County of Cornwall, were feloniously assaulted and obstructed by a large Body of Smugglers armed with Fire-arms and other offensive Weapons, who fired upon the said John Smith, and his crew, and succeeded in conveying the Smuggled Goods on board the said Vessel, on shore.

The Commissioners of His Majesty's Customs, in order to bring to Justice any one or more of the said offenders, are hereby pleased to offer

A REWARD OF
£200

to any Person or Persons who will discover and apprehend, or cause to be discovered and apprehended, the said offenders, to be paid by the Collector of His Majesty's Customs at the port of Falmouth, upon conviction.

By order of the Commissioners,
GEORGE DELAVAUD,
Secretary.

ANNO QUADRAGESIMO QUINTO

GEORGII III. REGIS.

C A P. CXXI.

An Act for the more effectual Prevention of Smuggling.
[12th *July* 1805.]

WHEREAS in Defiance of the several Laws of Customs and Excise, great Quantities of Goods are illegally imported into, and landed in the United Kingdom, as well by clandestine Means as by open Force, to the great Detriment of the Revenue, and the Subversion of all Civil Authority: And whereas it is become highly necessary that some further Provision should be made for the Remedy of these great Evils: Be it therefore enacted by the King's most Excellent Majesty, by and with the Advice and Consent of the Lords Spiritual and Temporal, and Commons, in this present Parliament assembled, and by the Authority of the same, That, from and after the passing of this Act, if any Vessel or Boat coming from Foreign Parts, and belonging wholly or in Part to His Majesty's Subjects, or whereof One Half of the Persons on board shall be Subjects of His Majesty, (other than and except any Ship or other square-rigged Vessel), shall be found in any Part of the *British* or *Irish* Channels, or elsewhere on the High Seas, within One hundred Leagues of any Part of the Coasts of *Great Britain* or *Ireland*, or shall be discovered to have been within the said Limits, having on board any Foreign Brandy, Rum, Geneva, or other Spirits, in any Cask or Package of less Size or Content
16 Z

Above left: A notice placed in newspapers by the Customs commissioners offering a reward of £200 for information following the assault of Revenue officers in Mevagissey.

Above right: Prevention of Smuggling Act 1805.

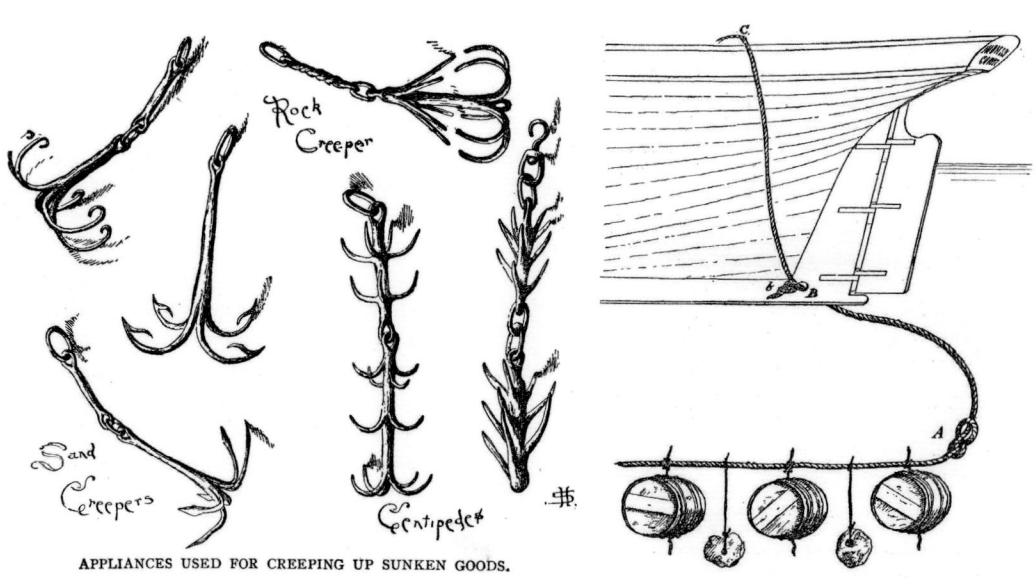

A moonlit Cornish coast, perfect conditions for the smugglers.

APPLIANCES USED FOR CREEPING UP SUNKEN GOODS.

Above left, right and page 28: Method of slinging tubs. Sketches by Lieut. Henry Shore RN from his book *Smuggling Days and Smuggling Ways*, published in 1892, showing the various methods used by smugglers to transport brandy, gin and rum. Shore held a senior position in the coastguard service at Fowey in the 1870s.

Nineteenth Century

Although the 'trade' had been flourishing in Cornwall for well over two centuries, it was not until the early part of the nineteenth century that a marked change came about, largely as a result of a determined attempt by the authorities to put an end to the smuggling that had been so openly carried on there for decades. The end of the Napoleonic wars freed large numbers of men and vessels belonging to the Navy to form the newly created Preventive and Coastguard services, and the aftermath of the *Lottery* incident in 1798, when a Customs officer was killed in the course of duty, led to a more clandestine behaviour by the smugglers.

The increasing vigilance of the coastguard drove the smugglers further away from the coast, and large quantities of contraband goods were sunk as far out as the Eddystone lighthouse off south Cornwall, where the reef proved a favourite location for sinking ankers of spirit.

West Briton & Cornwall Advertiser
2 January 1818

On Thursday last, the *Hind* and *Dolphin* revenue cutters, with the preventative boat stationed at King's Cove, Mount's Bay, got up between 90 and 100 kegs of foreign spirits which had been sunk by smugglers near Mullion.

METHOD OF SECURING TUBS AND STONES FOR SINKING.

A CROP SUNK.

Method of Slinging Tubs

Revenue vessel in pursuit of lugger.

Cornish fishermen in the nineteenth century ... how many of them were smugglers?

In Memory of John Perry Mariner
Who was unfortunately kill'd by a Cannon
Ball. by a Person unknown
In ÿ year 1779 Aged 24 years. June ÿ 5

John Perry's tombstone in Lansallos church yard.

Revenue cutter.

The Revenue Vessels

It was a dangerous, violent time for the crews of Revenue vessels operating off the Cornish coast, as indeed it was for smuggling craft. The possibility of mistaken identity was always present.

In the summer of 1799, John Perry, a member of a Polperro smuggling family, was shot while in a boat off the south coast of Cornwall. Perry left a widow and a small child, and John Quiller of Polperro, perhaps leader of the smuggling syndicate, decided he would try to get the perpetrator brought to justice. He was certain that the shot had come from a London privateer called the *Betsey* (probably involved in the same Guernsey trade). Quiller put an advertisement in the *Sherborne Mercury* in August 1799, alleging that the *Betsey's* then captain had 'fired upon a boat's crew near Polperro, and killed a poor inoffensive man immediately, who has left a poor widow with many small children.' He offered a reward of 10 guineas to anyone who would apprehend the captain.

There is a long catalogue of known seizures of goods suspected – usually correctly – to be smuggled. Some of them concern the Revenue cruisers which operated along the coast, others Royal Naval vessels passing on convoy and other coastwise duty, as well as the men of the 'land-guard'. Many of them amply justify the reputation of Cornish smugglers as tough, adventurous and sometimes ruthless men.

Naval vessels and their crews were equally active offshore, trying to intercept the smugglers' cargoes offshore before they were landed.

In April 1783 the sloop HMS *Beaver*, commanded by Lieutenant Joseph Peyton, was off Lundy Island when it came across and seized a large smuggling lugger named the *Swallow*. Peyton may not at first have realised the outstanding history of the Guernsey-owned *Swallow* as a former privateer from Polperro. Her master at this date was William Johns, who had taken over from John Quiller in the previous year. Not surprisingly, she was not caught without a lively chase which lasted 6 hours. The *Beaver* had spotted the lugger lying at anchor in Lundy Road on the evening of 17 April. The following morning, the lugger had cut her cable and was trying to escape when Peyton fired several guns to bring her to. Without a breath of wind to assist them, the Polperro crew stood little chance of escaping the heavily armed sloop being steadily hauled towards them by its crew and boats; after about 6 hours of desperately pulling on the lugger's sweeps they were eventually overhauled and boarded without a fight.

The *Swallow* was loaded with 119 sacks of Bohea tea, 242 barrels of brandy and 90 barrels of gin, altogether worth nearly £2,000. Since no papers could be produced to account for such a cargo, it was correctly assumed to be contraband. Caught in the very act of smuggling, crew, cargo and vessel were impounded by the *Beaver* and ordered to sail under escort for Plymouth the following day. If the profits from smuggling were large, so too were the risks and losses. The loss of the *Swallow* and her valuable cargo was a severe blow to the lugger's owners who included Zephaniah Job, the notorious Polperro 'smugglers' banker'.

If the Revenue officers on land were being frustrated in their attempts to put an end to the smuggling trade, the Revenue cutters at sea met with rather more success. One Revenue vessel in particular came to be feared by the Cornish smugglers more than any other. The *Hind*, one of the newest and largest cutters in service, carrying a crew of forty-one men, was stationed in the Channel between Portland and Land's End. Like other Revenue cutters in service at the time, the *Hind* was a former smuggling lugger seized off Plymouth in January 1789 and judged too useful to suffer the usual fate and be broken up. Instead, she was converted into a cutter and taken into service. Broad beamed, with little freeboard, her low deck level was compensated for by high red painted bulwarks into which gun ports had been cut. Her sixteen carriage guns on the gun deck were of the new carronade type. As well as the carriage guns, the *Hind* carried a swivel gun in the stern. The small boats on her deck were used for boarding and patrol work inshore. At sea, with her large gaff mainsail, double square topsails and large jib set, she presented a daunting sight to any Polperro lugger plying between Guernsey and the Cornish coast.

Her commander, Lieutenant Gabriel Bray, had served aboard Revenue cutters since 1779 with a zeal and determination that won the admiration of his superiors and gained him a reputation for dealing ruthlessly with smugglers. A few years earlier, while in command of the Revenue cutter *Scourge* off the Kent coast, Bray had confronted a notorious smuggler named Brown in the act of landing spirits on the beach near Deal.

It was not long before Gabriel Bray made his presence felt in Cornwall, where the Revenue officials at Fowey were quick to enlist his help in putting an end to the trade so openly carried on in the area. Bray led another raid in 1797 after receiving a tip-off that a large number of casks of liquor were about to be landed near Polperro and hidden in the cellar of a local fisherman, William Minards. Knowing that surprise was vital if he was to impound the goods before they were moved, Bray ordered the *Hind*'s second officer, Hugh Pearce, to approach Polperro from the sea with two boatloads of armed crewmen while he made his way overland from Polruan. On the way, Bray called at the rectory at Lansallos to obtain a search warrant from the Reverend Charles Kendall before continuing on to Polperro where he met up with Pearce and the boat party who had already arrived outside Minard's cellar. Leaving the *Hind* crewmen to guard the spot where the kegs were stored, Bray and his second officer went in search of a constable.

Unable to find one, the two men returned to find a large crowd gathering angrily outside the cellar led by Richard Rowett, his cousin Benjamin Rowett and brother-in-law Reginald Barrett claiming that no Custom House officer had a right to seize anything on shore. The ensuing scene was reminiscent of Llewyn's earlier attempt to seize contraband goods there. In Bray's absence, some of the mob had entered the cellar and were preparing to carry off the casks inside when two of the *Hind*'s crew, John Hawkins and Richard Verran, attempted to stop them. Verran grabbed a cask from the shoulder of one man but as he did so, both he and Hawkins were set upon and manhandled out of the cellar by the crowd, now rapidly swelling in number as news of the raid spread through Polperro. Outside, Hugh Pearce found himself thrust up against the wall of the building by Richard Rowett, who grabbed him by the collar and threatened to beat his brains out. At the same time, Benjamin Rowett warned he would shoot the first man to lay a hand on the cellar door while his fellow smugglers removed the kegs inside. When Gabriel Bray and his crew eventually did succeed in entering the cellar with the aid of a detachment of Lancashire Militia, they found most of the kegs had been removed or destroyed.

Infuriated at being thwarted yet again, Gabriel Bray determined that the ringleaders should be brought to justice for their part in the affray. Warrants were issued for the arrest of four Polperro men who had been positively identified as having prevented the Revenue officers from seizing the goods: the two Rowett cousins, Richard and Benjamin, together with Reginald Barrett and John Minards, son of the owner of the cellar where the liquor had been stored.

Although charges of armed assault and obstruction against all four were read out at a court hearing at Westminster in June 1799, the case was never proceeded with. Had Zephaniah Job intervened yet again on behalf of the Polperro smugglers? If so, it was one of the last occasions he was able to use his influence to prevent justice from taking its course.

Gabriel Bray, determined to put a stop to the smuggling trade at Polperro, was soon to take a decisive role in the Revenue service's efforts to suppress it.

A Revenue cutter in pursuit of a smuggling lugger.

A contemporary full hull model of the *Hawke* (active 1777) – a Revenue cutter, built plank on frame using clinker construction in the Georgian style. The model is decked, fully equipped and rigged with a full suit of original sails set. (© National Maritime Museum, Greenwich, London)

Polperro harbour at the end of the eighteenth century.

The Smugglers

It is not always clear who the smugglers' 'retail' customers were, though Cornish innkeepers must have provided a steady trade.

Jamaica Inn, made famous by Daphne du Maurier's novel, may well have been one such location, but what is more certain is that most of the inns at ports around the coast of Cornwall where contraband was brought ashore would have provided a ready market.

The Polperro smugglers went as far as Land's End to market their goods, and one such expedition ended in disaster in 1804. On Sunday 4 November a smuggling lugger lay off Porth Just Cove, at St Just in Penwith. Eight men set off for the shore in a boat, but within 20 yards of the shore it was overturned by a heavy surf. Only three of the eight were saved. The *Sherborne Mercury* reported:

> The unfortunate sufferers were chiefly young men belonging to the lugger, and inhabitants of Polperro. In the course of the day three bodies were washed ashore, and on Monday an inquest was taken by Mr. Rogers, the coroner, on their bodies, and verdicts of Accidental Death were of course returned. The names of the three men who were picked up were, Thomas Hicks, an innkeeper, of St. Just, about 27 years of age, who carried out with him bank and other bills to the amount of nearly 100 and when he was taken up about 90 were found and preserved; Richard Toms, a young man of 19, belonging to Polperro, and also Richard Richards, of the same place, who it is hoped, has left only a widow to lament his untimely end.

Polperro harbour, photographed by Lewis Harding *c.* 1870.

The same view today.

One of the hundreds of beer houses or kiddleywinks found throughout Cornwall in earlier centuries. Although licensed only to sell beer, other cheap liquor was sold, much of it having been smuggled into the county from France.

An early nineteenth century oil painting of Polperro harbour by the English landscape artist William Linton, *c.* 1820.

The Three Pilchards Inn by Polperro harbour, a favourite haunt for local smugglers. When Charles Jolliff (1807–1887) was the landlord, the sight of him saddling his horse late at night was a sure sign that there were 'goods' to be delivered.

Polperro

No account of smuggling in Cornwall would be complete without reference to Polperro, the fishing port between Looe and Fowey on the south coast. Its very isolation and landlocked location made it an ideal haven for contraband goods to be brought ashore there during the eighteenth century by local fishermen and others, but the arrival of Zephaniah Job, the notorious 'smugglers' banker', in the 1770s was to turn the smuggling trade from a cottage industry into a highly lucrative business on a scale unrivalled elsewhere.

Dr Jonathan Couch, in his *History of Polperro* published in 1871, wrote:

> Our town was probably a stronghold of the contraband trade in early times. All joined in it; the smith left his forge, and the husbandman his plough; even women and children turned out to assist in the unlawful traffic, and received their share of the proceeds. That it was in any degree a dishonest pursuit perhaps never entered their minds; and if it did, they saw enough in the conduct of those above them to satisfy less unscrupulous minds that theirs was a venial offence. The gentry of the neighbourhood bought their brandy and lace; the excise and custom-house officers connived in unlawful acts, and profited by secret connection with the smugglers. Revenue cruisers were not infrequently detected with contraband goods on board, and sometimes caught in the act.

Sheer economic necessity drove the Polperro seafarers to smuggling. If the pilchard shoals failed to arrive off the coast during the summer and autumn months, or storms prevented the boats from putting to sea, everyone shared the hardship and hunger of a bleak winter ahead. As a result, generations of fishermen there had supplemented their living by bringing contraband ashore, often at secluded coves along the coast near Polperro under cover of darkness.

The Quiller family were particularly notorious for their smuggling activities during the latter half of the eighteenth century. William Quiller was aged just twenty-two when he was in command of the *Vigilant*, a fishing boat belonging to his father, which was seized by the Revenue cutter *Constitution* during the night of 14 June 1797. The *Constitution*'s commander, Lieutenant John Weston, had good reason to suspect that a Polperro boat was quite likely to be carrying more than just a cargo of fish, but on this occasion he was

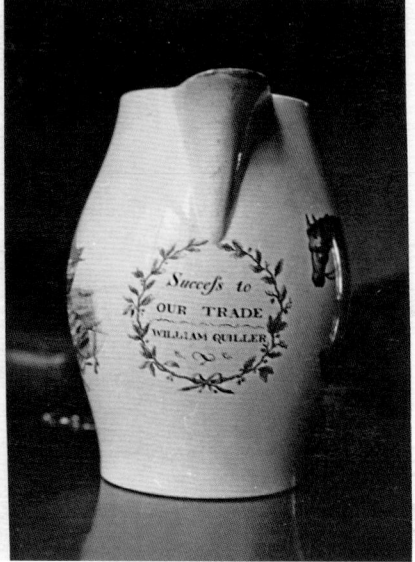

William Quiller's 'smuggling' jug showing a lugger on one side and a packhorse laden with barrels on the other, and the traditional toast of the Cornish smugglers: 'Success to Our Trade'.

unlucky. Although no contraband goods were found aboard her, the *Vigilant* was brought into Falmouth under escort.

The Quillers were already in trouble with the law at that time since both William and his father John had been ordered to stand trial in London along with Richard Oliver, charged with possessing contraband. Zephaniah Job intervened on their behalf, doing his utmost to discredit the principal witness for the prosecution, a local man named Robert Coath. 'If this rascal was not to be silenced he would ruin every smuggler in this place,' he told the Guernsey dealers Nicholas Maingy and Brothers in November 1797, adding that he had arranged for several farmers in the Polperro neighbourhood to testify that Coath was a liar:

> I hope these men will invalidate Coath's evidence and that Messrs Quiller and Oliver will get through this unpleasant business. Should credit be given to Coath's evidence Oliver & Co. would be fined heavy for the goods seized in a cellar – which I hope however they will not.

But the tragic outcome of the *Lottery* incident in 1798 was to mark the end of the golden age of the 'trade' through Polperro. The first Customs boat was stationed there in April 1801 and Zephaniah Job began to sever his links with the smuggling trade and concentrate instead on his banking and other commercial interests.

The Smugglers' Banker

That smuggling thrived on an almost industrial scale through Polperro during the latter half of the eighteenth century was almost entirely due to the presence of one man, Zephaniah Job.

Job had arrived there in the early 1770s as an educated young man who had been compelled to flee his home in west Cornwall and initially earned a living as a schoolmaster, teaching the sons of the local fishermen, many of whom were smugglers. He soon found himself acting as bookkeeper, general correspondent and advisor for the menfolk, most of whom were illiterate. Generations of Polperro mariners had, like others around the coast of Cornwall, supplemented their living by bringing contraband ashore, often at secluded nearby coves under cover of darkness. Once landed on the beach, the illicit cargoes would quickly be taken away inland along well-trodden paths to secret hiding places where they could be stored safely before being distributed.

Most of the business Zephaniah Job conducted for nearly thirty years on behalf of the Polperro smugglers was with the four principal Guernsey merchant houses of Jersey & De Lisle (later Peter De Lisle & Sons), Nicholas Maingy & Brothers, John Lukis and Carteret Priaulx. Between 1787 and 1805, he had accounts with at least eight suppliers on the island who, with the exception of Carteret Priaulx & Co., dealt almost exclusively with him when supplying Polperro. The smugglers usually obtained their supplies from Guernsey on credit terms extending over several months, allowing them time to sell the goods. Job then collected payments from them, acting as guarantor, and forwarded the money to Guernsey, either directly or through one of his London agents. A discount of 10 per cent was often allowed for ready money – cash on delivery – as an added incentive for prompt payment. The St Peter Port merchants relied on his recommendation when dealing with the smugglers and he in turn would reassure them that those he represented were dependable.

Job's accounts for the period between 1788 and 1804 give some indication of the scale of the trade with Polperro. The sums he collected on behalf of just three of the Guernsey firms during that period amounted to nearly £100,000: £30,500 credited to Jersey & De Lisle between 1778 and 1789; a total of £23,000 to Carteret Priaulx between 1778 and 1799, and an astonishing £42,755 to the Maingy brothers. On average, the Polperro smugglers paid Job a total of nearly £6,000 a year over a twenty-year period.

When it came to dealing with the Guernsey merchants who supplied the smugglers, he at first added only 0.5 per cent on the money paid in to their credit by the Polperro smugglers; by 1782, he had increased this to 1 per cent, adding only the cost of postage. Although small sums of money were often sent in cash across by boat to the Guernsey firms, a substantial proportion was transferred through various London banking houses and agents with whom Job had accounts often running to several thousands of pounds at a time.

Although Job became known as the smugglers' banker, most of the smugglers did not in fact bank with him. His role was to receive their payments on account of the Guernsey dealers and to remit these, so that he was more of a banker to the Guernsey traders than to the smugglers who were given several months credit from the time the goods were shipped until payment for them was due. The extent to which the suppliers relied on Job to indicate who they could safely supply goods to was an essential part of the trust on which their dealings with the smugglers was based.

The banknotes issued by Job were among the first to be circulated in Cornwall, but he was always careful to observe the essential condition of having sufficient cash available in exchange for his paper money. The custom of issuing paper money had originated during the wars with France when the enormous cost of the military effort drastically reduced the amount of gold and silver coinage in circulation. Bank of England notes were declared legal tender and occasionally Job found his creditors preferring them to his own, as in 1819 when he was obliged to exchange six Bank of England £1 notes for his own, observing: 'I have the satisfaction to know that my notes are readily received by every banker in the country and by every respectable merchant and shopkeeper.'

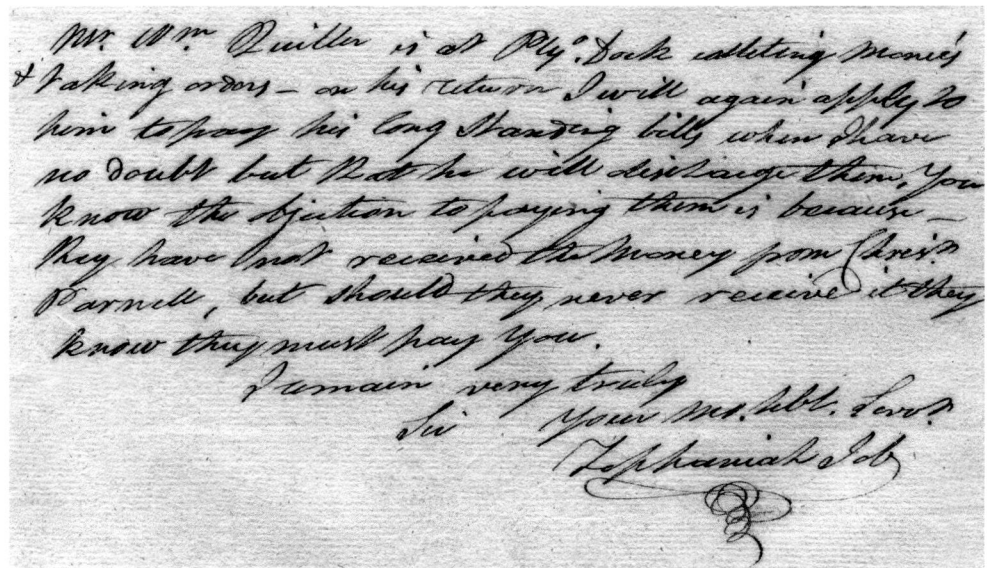

A letter from Zephaniah Job.

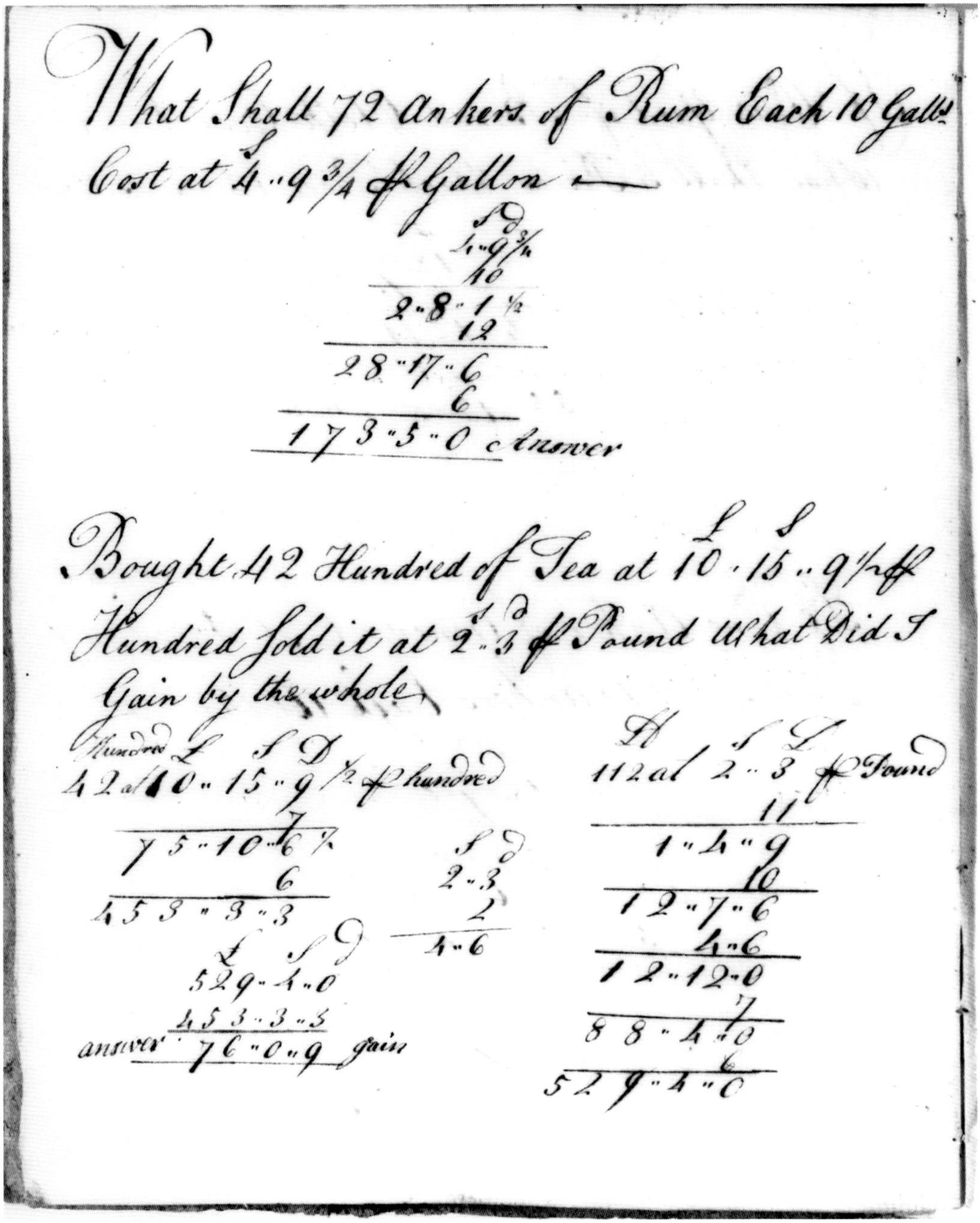

What shall 72 Ankers of Rum Each 10 Gall.
Cost at £4..9¾ ⅌ Gallon —

$$
\begin{array}{l}
£\quad s\quad d \\
4..9¾ \\
10 \\
\hline
2..8..1½ \\
12 \\
\hline
28..17..6 \\
6 \\
\hline
173..5..0\quad \text{Answer}
\end{array}
$$

Bought 42 Hundred of Tea at £10..15..9½ ⅌
Hundred sold it at 2..3 ⅌ Pound What Did I
Gain by the whole.

Hundred £ s D
42 at 10..15..9½ ⅌ hundred

$$
\begin{array}{l}
7\;5..10..6¾ \\
6 \\
\hline
453..3..3 \\
\\
529..4..0 \\
453..3..3 \\
\hline
\text{answer}\;\;76..0..9\quad \text{gain}
\end{array}
$$

£ s
112 at 2..3 ⅌ Pound

$$
\begin{array}{l}
11 \\
\hline
1..4..9 \\
10 \\
\hline
12..7..6 \\
4..6 \\
\hline
12..12..0 \\
7 \\
\hline
88..4..0 \\
6 \\
\hline
529..4..0
\end{array}
$$

A page from the schoolbook of John Clements, one of Zephaniah Job's pupils in Polperro in the 1770s. The calculations he set his pupils reflected the trade in contraband goods carried on by their fathers: 'What shall 72 ankers of Rum each 10 gallons cost at £4.9¾ per gallon.'

A double-page extract from one of Zephaniah Job's ledgers for 1794, revealing the payments received from the smugglers and the large sums of money remitted to the Guernsey merchants via their London agents. (Royal Institution of Cornwall)

Polperro £1 banknote.

44

A lugger.

After his death at the age of seventy-three in January 1822, Zephaniah Job's estate was valued at £7,766; though he left no will, there was more than enough cash at his premises in Polperro to honour all the promissory notes on his bank in circulation. Most of his ledgers and account books were destroyed by fire shortly after his death, possibly to destroy any incriminating evidence, but a few survived to be discovered some eighty years later, hidden in a worm-eaten chest at Crumplehorn Mill above Polperro.

Left: Zephaniah Job's ledgers.

Below: Plymouth Sound map.

The *Lottery*

Even in the heyday of West Country smuggling, the murder of a Revenue officer was rare enough. But an event occurred one winter's night in 1798 that was to have far-reaching consequences in Cornwall and mark the eventual decline in the contraband trade there.

The story began on Boxing Day evening. War with France had been continuous for the past six years, but had little or no effect on the trade in uncustomed French spirits, which were bought in Guernsey and landed on the Cornish coast. This traffic was largely in the hands of smuggling syndicates from ports like Looe, Polperro and Fowey, supplied by Guernsey merchants and financed by Zephaniah Job and perhaps others of his ilk in Cornwall.

On this moonlight evening of Wednesday 26 December, the *Lottery*, a large cutter, was approaching the south-eastern coast of Cornwall. She had a substantial cargo of contraband to be landed at Cawsand Bay. Customs kept a six-oared preventive boat stationed at Cawsand, manned on this occasion by four oarsmen under the 'Sitter', a man named Ambrose Bowden who had received a tip-off that the *Lottery* was to land a cargo consisting mainly of spirits and tobacco.

Bowden told his men to row towards Penlee Point, the south-western boundary of Cawsand Bay, separating it from the longer Whitsand Bay to the west where they spotted the *Lottery* at anchor.

As they got nearer, he saw several boats lying alongside of her and at her stern: evidently to land a smuggled cargo. When the Customs boat had got to within about 100 yards of the cutter, someone on board hailed it. Bowden replied that his was a king's boat. At this someone in the cutter called out: 'Keep off, you buggers, or I will fire into you'. Bowden again said that his was a king's boat, and a Revenue boat, and dared the people on board to fire.

During this exchange Bowden was standing up in the boat, with the Revenue flag in his hand, when men on board the *Lottery* again shouted to the Customs men to keep off, and themselves fired three times with guns. One of the oarsmen, Humphrey Glinn, slumped forward, hit by the firing from the *Lottery* – the front of his head being blown off. Bowden returned fire with several shots of his musket. The cutter's crew then cut their cable and sailed away westward, continuing to fire over her stern at the Revenue

Lottery.

WHEREAS it has been humbly represented to the King, that RICHARD OLIVER,
the Younger, RICHARD BARRETT, the Younger,
WILLIAM SWARTMAN, the Younger, PHILIP
LIBBY, the Younger, THOMAS GEORGE, and RO-
GER TOMS, of Polperrow, in the county of Cornwall,
mariners, and lately belonging to a smuggling vessel called
the Lottery, stand charged upon oath with being concerned
in the WILFUL MURDER of HUMPHRY GLINN,
late a boatman belonging to the six-oared boat in the service of the Customs, stationed at Cawsand, on the 26th of
December last, between the hours of ten and eleven at
night, off Penlee Point, on the coast of Cornwall, by
firing from on board the said vessel called the Lottery with
muskets at the said boat.

His Majesty, for the better discovering and bringing to
justice the above-named persons, is hereby pleased to pro-
mise his most gracious pardon to any one of the said offenders, (except Richard Oliver, the younger, the master
of the said vessel, and Richard Barrett, the younger, one
of the owners thereof, and the persons who actually fired)
who shall discover his accomplice or accomplices, or be
the means of any one or more of them being apprehended
and committed to prison for the said offence.

PORTLAND.

And as a further encouragement, the Commissioners of
his Majesty's Customs do hereby offer a Reward of Two
Hundred Pounds to any one of the said offenders, (except
as before excepted) or to any other person or persons who
shall apprehend, or cause to be apprehended, any one or
more of them, the said Richard Oliver, the younger,
Richard Barrett, the younger, William Swartman, the
younger, Philip Libby, the younger, Thomas George,
and Roger Toms, whose descriptions are hereinafter mentioned ; which said reward will be paid by the Receiver-
General of the Customs, upon the said persons, or either
of them, being apprehended and committed to prison.

By order of the Commissioners,
J. HUME, Secretary.

Customs notice.

men. Bowden took Glinn to HMS *Stag*, a naval ship anchored in Cawsand Bay, where he was pronounced dead.

As always when an officer of the law is killed on duty, the authorities were understandably determined to catch the culprits and make an example of them. Every Revenue cruiser was on constant watch for the *Lottery*, but not a trace of her could be found. The Customs commissioners took the unusual step of authorising a reward of £200 for the capture of those concerned, with a royal pardon to any of the offenders except the master or commander of the *Lottery* and the person or persons who actually fired, who would inform on their accomplices. The reward and pardon were advertised in the *Sherborne Mercury* and *Exeter Gazette* and a large number of handbills were distributed in Cornwall.

The *Lottery*'s luck finally ran out on the afternoon of Monday 13 May, when she was sighted off Start Point on the Devon coast by Gabriel Bray, in command of the *Hind* Revenue cutter. Bray at once set off in pursuit, doggedly following the *Lottery* as she tacked close in and out along the shore in a desperate attempt to escape. After a chase that lasted through the night and into the following afternoon, the two vessels were finally becalmed off Land's End where, after a brief skirmish, the *Lottery* and her crew of seventeen were seized as they abandoned the vessel and made for the shore. The following day they were brought into Plymouth along with the cargo of brandy, gin, tea and tobacco found aboard her at the time.

One of those taken aboard the *Hind* was a Polperro man named Roger Toms, who had been on board the *Lottery* when Humphry Glinn was killed. In order to gain a pardon for himself, Toms agreed to testify against those of his fellow crewmen who had been involved. He named another Polperro man, Thomas Potter, as having fired the fatal shot. As Potter was not among those captured by the *Hind*, Captain Bray wasted no time on arrival at Plymouth rounding up a party of dragoons and set off overland to Polperro. Arriving there by stealth at midnight, they were able to surprise Potter at home in bed and bring the startled man back to Plymouth, where he was confined in the notorious 'Black Hole' dungeon in Devonport for three days before being formally charged with the murder of Glinn and taken eventually to Newgate gaol in London.

Two of the other prisoners captured by the *Hind*, William Searle and Thomas Ventin, were also named by Roger Toms as having been implicated in the murder of Glinn. The remaining *Lottery* crewmen were prosecuted and convicted for smuggling; five were also charged with armed resistance and tried at the Old Bailey, where they were sentenced to two years' hard labour aboard the *Stanislas*, one of the leaking, rat-infested prison hulks moored on the Thames at Woolwich.

Toms, a key prosecution witness in the case against Potter, Searle and Ventin, was allowed to go free but, for his own safety, was made a member of the *Hind*'s crew. His freedom was short lived, however. Just two weeks later, while the *Hind* lay at anchor in the Fowey estuary, Toms' wife Martha was persuaded to go to Polruan for a secret rendezvous with her husband.

As the couple walked together across the downs above Lantic Bay nearby, a group of Polperro men lying in wait seized Toms, carrying him off and shipping him across to Guernsey where he was held. Without him, the case against Tom Potter, Searle and Ventin could not proceed and the trial at the Old Bailey was postponed. Undeterred by the loss

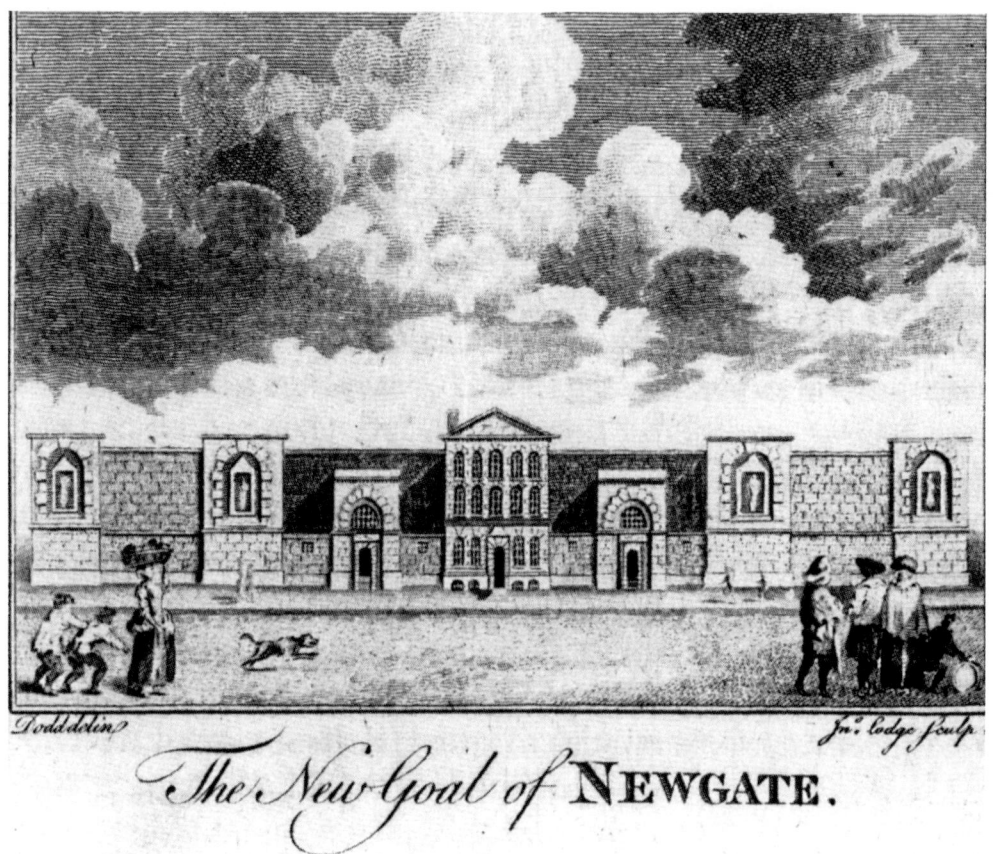

The New Goal of NEWGATE.

Newgate.

of their key witness, the authorities were still determined to prosecute the case against all the men.

The names of six missing men and their descriptions were published, including that of Roger Toms, described as having 'a very dark complexion, long face, balding with short curly black hair, about five feet six inches in height, of middling stature and has a rupture.' Although his age was given as forty-five, he was in fact only forty-one years old. A reward of £200 was offered to anyone giving information leading to the arrest of any of the others named: Richard Oliver, the *Lottery*'s commander, described as 'about 6 feet high, rather thin but very boney and walks very upright'; Richard Barrett, 'about 32 years of age, very thin and rather stoops in his walk'; Philip Libby, 'about 42 years of age, very stout'; William Swartman, 'about 24 years of age, long brown tied hair' and Thomas George, 'long thin face, very wide mouth, short black hair, rather bald, about 50 years of age and has lost part of the fore finger of one of his hands.'

Such detailed descriptions could only have been provided by Roger Toms, who was eventually found the following year in Guernsey, having been identified in St Peter Port. Returned to Plymouth aboard the Revenue cutter *Swift* in April 1800, Toms was taken at once under military escort to Exeter gaol where he was again interviewed by Gabriel Bray, intent on learning the whereabouts of the remaining members of the *Lottery* crew still at large, probably on Guernsey.

With their principal witness now safely returned, the authorities wasted little time bringing the case against Thomas Potter, William Searle and Thomas Ventin for the murder of Humphry Glinn at the Old Bailey early in June. Two other key prosecution witnesses, Ambrose Bowden, the Customs officer whose boat had intercepted the *Lottery* off Cawsand, and Hugh Pearce, first officer of the *Hind* at the time the *Lottery* crew were taken prisoner, set off by coach together from Plymouth on 4 June to attend the trial in London. Bowden was taken ill at the outset, however, and by the time he had reached Exeter he was feeling so unwell that he was unable to travel on any further. He did eventually recover sufficiently to travel on as far as Egham in Surrey where, four days later, he lay so seriously ill at the Kings Head Inn that a local doctor certified that he could not possibly continue the journey to London 'without imminent danger to his life.' In the face of such medical evidence and the absence of such an important witness, the prosecution had little option but to ask once again for the trial to be postponed until the Customs officer from Cawsand was well enough to attend and give evidence.

Was Bowden's mysterious and sudden illness genuine, or had he been got at? Back at Polperro, Zephaniah Job later secretly recorded a curious series of payments in connection with the *Lottery* trial, including one payment of £105 to Ambrose Bowden dated 7 June 1800, just two days before he was lying so dangerously ill at Egham. Perhaps Bowden had been bribed to swallow some toxic substance that induced the symptoms that prevented his appearance at the Old Bailey? It was certainly a very large sum of money to be giving one of the key prosecution witnesses in a murder trial involving the Polperro smugglers. Another item entered by Job records a further £112 on 'expence to and from London' in June that year, no doubt in connection with the trial. Whatever the reason for Bowden's indisposition, it did no more than delay the eventual trial for a further six months until December when, nearly two years after Glinn's murder, the three former *Lottery* crewmen appeared once more together in the dock at the Old Bailey.

The most damning evidence was given by Roger Toms, who admitted being aboard the *Lottery* on the night in question and named the prisoners Potter, Searle and Ventin as well as those still sought in connection with Glinn's murder, including Richard Oliver, Richard Barrett, William Swartman, Philip Libby, Thomas George and a man known as Irish Jack as being on board at the time.

The main effort of the defence counsel was aimed at discrediting Toms and several witnesses were called to swear they knew him to be a liar and a thief. They, in turn, were closely cross-examined by the prosecuting counsel, intent on showing that they, as well as everyone else living near the coast, were smugglers and therefore interested in protecting the prisoners. The Admiralty judge, Sir William Scott, summed up by telling the jury of twelve men that everyone on board the *Lottery* at the time the shot that killed Humphry Glinn was fired was equally as guilty as the person who fired it. The question the jury had to decide was whether the prisoners were on board at the time, and that depended on the evidence of Roger Toms.

After retiring for nearly an hour, the jury returned a verdict of guilty against Thomas Potter for the murder of the Customs officer. Although William Searle and Thomas Ventin were acquitted of murder, they were nevertheless sentenced to the same two years

A PIRATE hanged at Execution Dock.

Execution Dock.

hard labour on the Thames as the other members of the *Lottery*'s crew. The judge then pronounced the death sentence in the prescribed manner, addressing Potter at length and concluding with the macabre words: 'You will be conveyed to the place of execution on Friday next, and there hanged by the neck until you shall be dead, and your body afterwards given to be dissected and anatomised.'

Due to the unusually high tide on the Thames at the time, the wretched Potter was kept in one of the condemned cells at Newgate until the following week when, on Thursday 18 December, he was taken on the 2-mile journey by horse-drawn cart to Execution Dock at Wapping accompanied by the prison chaplain. There, at the turn of the tide, Tom Potter met his death at the age of twenty-six on the gallows set at low water mark by the customary method reserved for those convicted of crime on the high seas. An Irishman from county Waterford, he was attended by a Roman Catholic priest and, it was reported afterwards, conducted himself with great penitence.

The tragic outcome of the *Lottery*'s encounter with the Customs boat at Cawsand and the events that followed had far-reaching consequences for many of those involved. Despite efforts to conceal his involvement, it is now evident that Zephaniah Job went to considerable lengths to frustrate the prosecution of the case as well as do all he could to assist the unfortunate men captured by Captain Bray. In all, Job spent more than £700 in various payments to lawyers in London and other expenses in connection with the trial, including the mysterious payment of £105 to Ambrose Bowden just before her husband was due to testify against Potter in June 1800.

Smuggled goods coming ashore.

Roger Toms had good reason to fear for his life if he ever returned to Polperro after Potter's execution. Even his family rejected him and he remained at Newgate gaol for the rest of his life employed as an assistant turnkey.

Ambrose Bowden's courage in confronting the *Lottery* smugglers off Cawsand was rewarded with promotion to first officer aboard the Revenue cutter *Busy* at Plymouth in 1800. For Gabriel Bray, however, the capture of the *Lottery* was to be the ultimate success in his long campaign against the smugglers. Shortly after Potter's trial and execution, ill health compelled Bray to relinquish his command of the *Hind* after a career spanning nearly thirty years in the king's service at sea.

Peak Rock at the entrance to Polperro harbour, a familiar landmark to the smugglers.

Cawsand beach and cellars, 1910.

Cawsand

The location of the twin fishing villages of Cawsand and Kingsand in Cawsand Bay at the western entrance to Plymouth Sound, and their proximity to a ready market for the sale of French brandy, tobacco and other goods to wealthy customers in nearby Plymouth, meant that smuggling inevitably prospered there. The Cawsand smugglers employed a special kind of boat, six- and eight-oared galleys of light construction and great speed, ostensibly built for the fishing industry.

The activities of the Cawsand men were not confined to their own neighbourhood, however; they often ventured to west Cornwall and 'ran' cargoes as far as Padstow on the north coast. But much of their activity was confined to the stretch of coast that lies between the entrance to Plymouth harbour and Looe Island to the west, despite the presence of a large staff of Customs officers based in the area.

West Briton & Cornwall Advertiser
10 July 1829

On Saturday evening last, about eight o'clock, Mr Foot of the preventive waterguard at Cawsand, captured a sprit sail boat called the *Five Sisters* belonging to Cawsan with 98 tubs of foreign brandy and geneva on board, together with three men and boy. The boat was first discovered by one of the preventive men on the look out from the hill, and conceiving her to be suspicious, he informed Mr Foot of the circumstance, when the latter accompanied by four men well armed took one of the pilot boats from the bay and proceeded towards the boat in the offing. The smugglers did not suspect the persons in the pilot boat of any design on them until they were close to them; but on perceiving who the intended visitants were, they immediately crowded all sail to effect their escape. This they were likely to effect when the preventive men shewed their colours and commenced firing musketry at the smugglers. The seventh shot fired cut away the sprit-sail halliards, when the main-sail fell and the pursuers came alongside and secured the boat with its cargo and crew.

Above: Looe Island, view from the mainland.

Below: Concealed compartment fitted to the smuggling vessel *Daniel & William*.

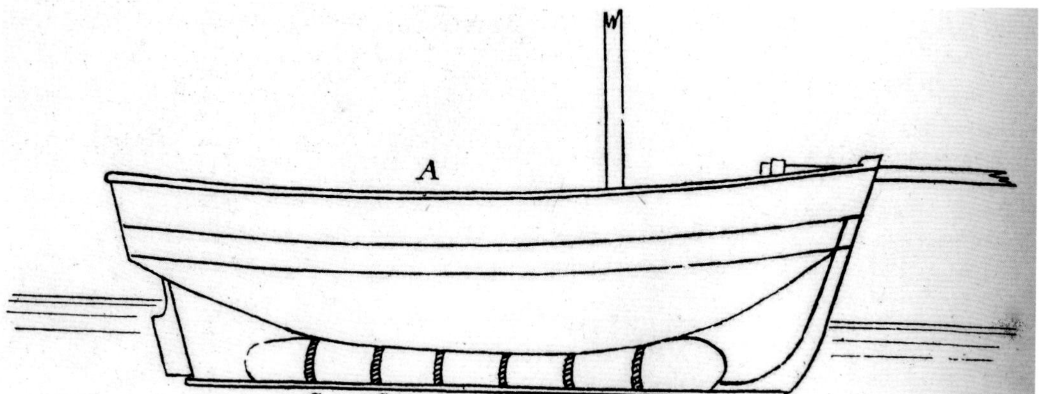

CONCEALMENT FITTED TO THE 'DANIEL AND WILLIAM'

Looe Island

Looe Island, with its coves, was an ideal staging post for landing and concealing goods until it was safe to ferry them to the mainland. The contraband included small casks of spirits known as 'tubs', tea, silk stockings and other goods subject to a high duty. In 1816, for example, the *West Briton & Cornwall Advertiser* reported that the cargo of a French vessel, that had to be assisted into Looe harbour after nearly running aground, included twelve toy horses in which were concealed some fifty-one pairs of silk stockings and nine silk shawls. Metal brackets still to be seen in the precipitous western cliffs of the island are thought to have been used to facilitate hauling contraband from sea level.

Looe Island became a haven for smuggled goods in the late eighteenth and early nineteenth century and one of the inhabitants, Amram Hooper, was to figure in the trade in the 1820s and 1830s. In 1834, a ship, the *Daniel & William*, carried spirits from France to Cornwall and these were landed on Looe Island, where Amram was living at the time at what is now called Smugglers Cottage. One of the secret stores was discovered in the twentieth century by accident, when someone fell through the floor of a cowshed.

A watch house was later constructed to accommodate an Excise officer and the 1851 census records that John Connor, commissioned boatman attached to Looe coastguard, was at the 'Coastguard Watch House' on the island.

Smugglers Cottage, Looe Island, once the home of Amram Hooper in the nineteenth century.

Smugglers hiding goods in a tomb.

Talland Bay

Talland Bay churchyard has been the resting place for many a smuggler, but in the past it was also used as a hiding place for contraband that had been brought ashore in the bay below. A lonely spot overlooking the sea where the ancient church stands alone within the sound of the waves, Talland has long been the source of ghost stories and tales of evil spirits. If there were spirits to be found there, they were almost certainly of an altogether different kind.

The Reverend Richard Doidge, vicar of Talland in the early eighteenth century, was an eccentric clergyman reputed to have great skills as an exorcist. One contemporary account describes how he would often be seen in the churchyard at night driving out 'evil spirits'. The likelihood was that this was a cover for local smugglers engaged in their highly profitable nocturnal business.

Ghosts or not, the coves and cliffs around Talland Bay were often frequented by folk engaged in running goods ashore under the cover of darkness, perhaps by moonlight. So prevalent was the trade that not even John Wesley's two visits to Polperro, the last in 1768, could persuade local Methodists to renounce their outlawed trade despite his preaching against it. On an earlier visit to Cornwall, Wesley recorded: 'An accursed thing among them: wellnigh one and all bought or sold uncustomed goods.'

Talland Bay cliffs.

Opposite above: Lansallos church, where many a smuggler is buried. From this lonely spot on the Cornish coast, a path leads down to the secluded Parson's Cove, where cargoes of contraband goods frequently came ashore.

Opposite below: A memorial inscription on the tower of Lansallos church, dedicated to William Johns (1740–1802) – a Polperro smuggler who was drowned near Land's End while trying to land a cargo of spirits.

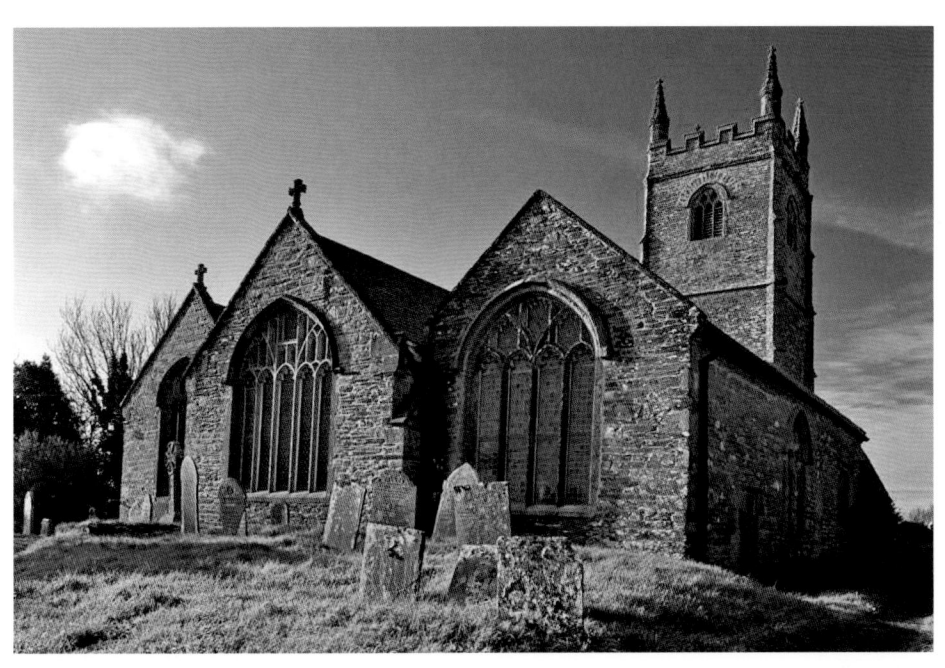

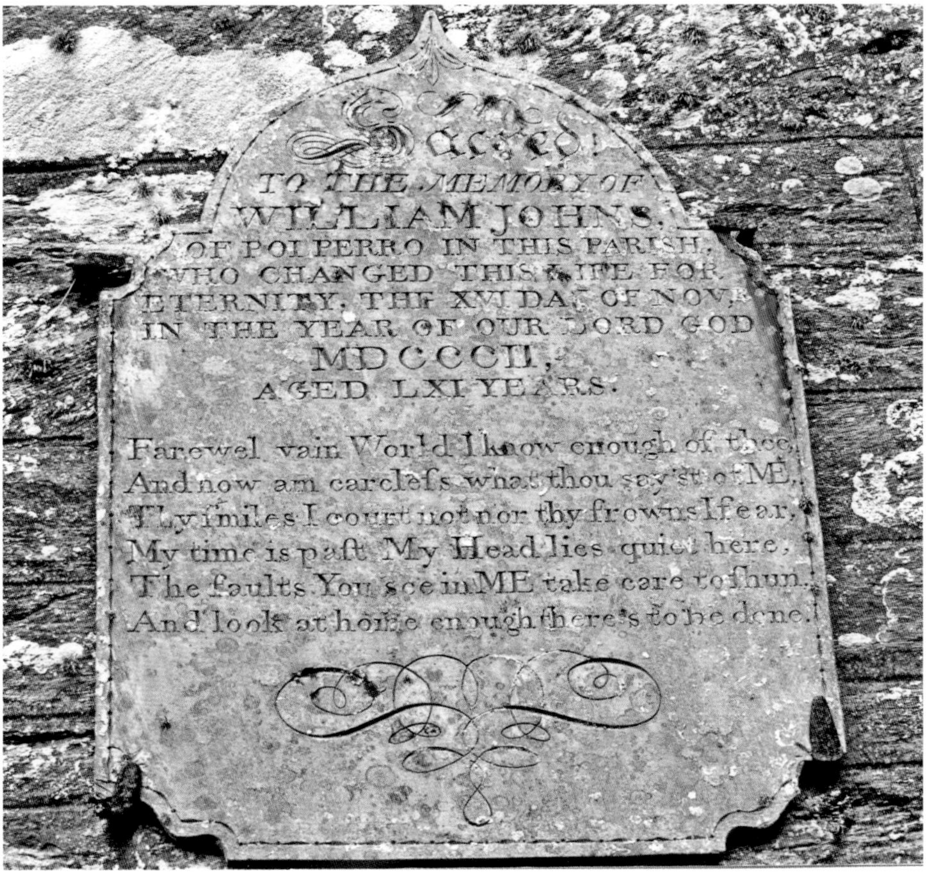
Sacred
TO THE MEMORY OF
WILLIAM JOHNS,
OF POLPERRO IN THIS PARISH,
WHO CHANGED THIS LIFE FOR
ETERNITY, THE XVI DAY OF NOV.
IN THE YEAR OF OUR LORD GOD
MDCCCII,
AGED LXI YEARS.
Farewel vain World I know enough of thee,
And now am carelefs what thou say'st of ME,
Thy fmiles I court not nor thy frowns I fear,
My time is paft My Head lies quiet here,
The faults You see in ME take care to fhun,
And look at home enough there's to be done.

Lantic Bay.

Lantic Bay

It was rare for a Cornish jury to return a verdict of guilty in cases involving smuggling. In March 1835, for example, a large gang of smugglers was caught red-handed by coastguard officers in possession of 118 tubs of spirits on the cliffs above Lantic Bay, a remote spot between Polperro and Fowey. Several of the smugglers were armed with sticks, and in the ensuing fight, five of the smugglers were taken prisoner and later charged with assault and being in possession of contraband goods. When the case against them was heard at the Cornwall Assizes in Bodmin in August, the jury, after a short consultation, returned a verdict of not guilty on the ground that the sticks produced as evidence could not be considered offensive weapons.

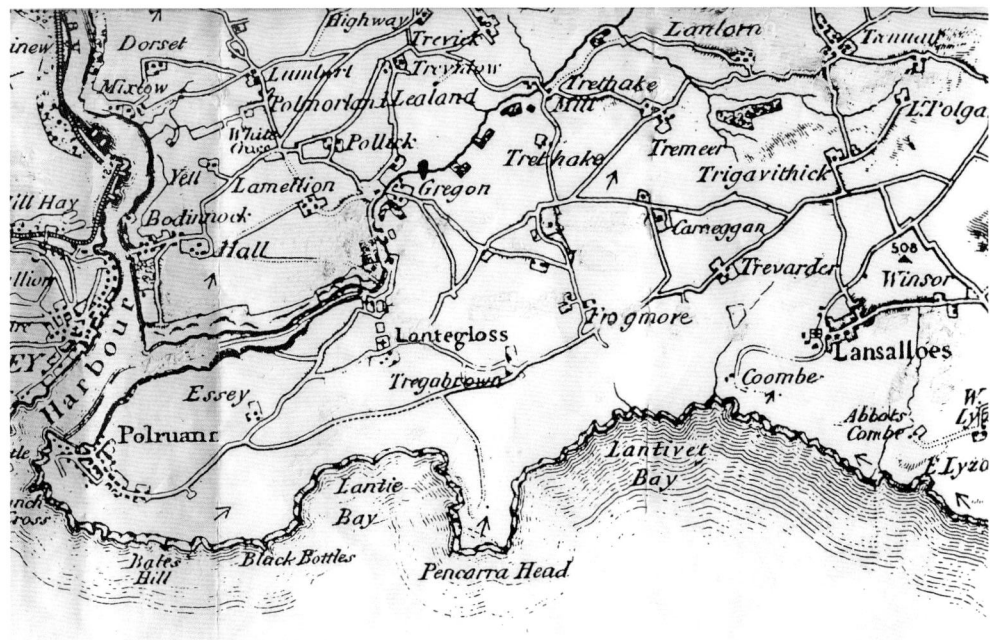

Lantic Bay map.

1805 map of the coast between Fowey and Looe.

A view of Fowey from Polruan.

Entrance to Fowey harbour.

Fowey

In spite of the penalties, some of the smugglers were bold enough to openly defy the Revenue officers. In April 1870, the *Hawke* in the service of Customs surprised the cutter *Active,* armed with ten carriage guns and eight swivel guns off Mevagissey. The *Active*'s master refused to allow an officer to board her, maintaining that his vessel was a privateer. Leaving a boat to watch the suspected smuggler, the *Hawke* made for Fowey and obtained permission to embark a sergeant, a corporal and twenty-two privates of the 1st Battalion Royals then stationed in the town. With these reinforcements he put out again and chased the *Active* along the coast. Shots were fired on either side but the sight of the 'red-coats' seems to have alarmed the cutter's men and they soon surrendered. When the *Active* was searched in Fowey harbour, 56 lbs of tea in small bags, one anker of geneva and fifty-seven pieces of chinaware were discovered and handed over to the Collector of Customs.

In the autumn of 1805 a Fowey lugger named the *Hope* was boarded by a Royal Navy frigate, HMS *Melampus*, some 5 miles off the Lizard. It was an unlucky encounter for the Cornishmen since their vessel had over 500 casks of spirits as well as bags of tobacco, pepper and salt below – all contraband. The lugger was, of course, seized, but the crew were offered the choice of standing trial as smugglers or volunteering in the Navy. With the exception of the master, all hands accepted the latter alternative and it was probably months, perhaps years, before they saw their families again.

Others were more fortunate than the crew of the *Hope*. Many made smuggling a profitable activity, even combining a smuggling trip with the more legitimate occupation of privateering.

Smuggling in this part of Cornwall certainly does not seem to have been accompanied by the violence that characterised it in other parts of Britain. It is true there was the *Lottery* affair in 1798 and as late as 1815, when the commander of the *Hind* Revenue cutter surprised a smuggling vessel in Mevagissey harbour and was about to take possession of her, only for smugglers to firedat the cutter's crew and in the confusion manage to get the goods safely on shore. In the winter of the following year John Horner and John Chubb, two riding officers in the service of HM Customs at the port of Fowey, met with a numerous gang of smugglers armed with firearms and other weapons and carrying on horses a large quantity of smuggled spirits in small casks at Polgooth in the parish of St Mewan. When the riding officers attempted to make a seizure the gang attacked them, dangerously wounded Horner and carried off his sword and pistol. A reward of £200 was offered to anyone giving information to the collector of Customs. These affrays invariably happened in some out of the way part where the smugglers had friends, for when in the same year the *Providence* Revenue cutter seized the open boat *James and Mary* in Fowey harbour, there seems to have been no resistance. There being no justice of the peace at Fowey on this occasion, the offenders were taken to Plymouth.

By 1830, however, determined efforts were being made by the authorities to put a stop to the contraband trade. The Revenue cutters sailed up and down the coast from Plymouth to Falmouth – at Fowey the *Hind* carried out this duty and was later replaced by the *Fox*, while ashore the Customs officers were assisted by riding officers who could call out a party of Dragoons if necessary to help them make a speedy capture. Finally a new force named the coastguard was formed to watch the actual coastline and patrol the cliffs and possible landing places. Prize money was held out as an inducement for making seizures and capturing smugglers. Stoppage of promotion threatened those who failed to prevent a 'run' being accomplished. Guernsey, so long a favourite rendezvous for the smuggling craft, had to be abandoned owing to new and crippling legislation, although Roscoff, situated on the Breton coast and therefore outside English law, took its place and for some years prospered by the change.

Ship Hotel, Fowey.

Careful and methodical planning was now imperative if these ventures were to succeed. The ringleader planned the 'runs', dealt with the merchants at Roscoff and with the buyers of the goods here in Cornwall, and arranged freights with the masters of the vessel bringing the cargoes across. Such a man was Richard Kingcup, who joined the coastguard at Polruan in 1824. He served four years as a commissioned boatman and then set up as publican at Fowey. For the next twenty years, during which time he moved to Plymouth and took over a shipbroking business, he was actively connected with smuggling enterprises. His every movement was carefully watched and noted by Customs.

There was certainly a very adequate system of gaining information and it led to many craft and their cargoes being seized. In 1824 the *Elizabeth* and *Grace* of Fowey were caught, while five years later the *Lucy* was seized at Chichester with 100 half-ankers of spirits concealed below. In 1832 a budget of news reached the Customs authorities from someone who was evidently in the know at Roscoff on the French coast. It was then reported that the *Rose* of Fowey, 11 tons, had taken across 100 tubs of brandy for Fowey and even then, with a larger vessel – the *Eagle*, of 35 tons – was loading a cargo for the same district. Early in the following year the *Eagle* paid two visits to this locality, the first time with 300 tubs and the second with 150 – she was evidently making some very successful trips. Another vessel, the *Love*, sailed for Fowey with 150 tubs aboard. It was certainly a more paying game than fishing, although if caught red-handed the penalties were severe; impressment into the Navy for five years and seizure of the goods. As for the boat, she might be taken over by Customs or deliberately sawn into three parts and sold as firewood. It was a risky business. On the *Eagle*'s last mentioned trip it was reported that she and two other craft had twice put back into Roscoff, having been chased by a Revenue cutter which had fired upon them. Only by good sailing did the *Eagle* manage to escape.

Finally there was the actual landing of the goods. The usual method was for the smuggling vessel to take advantage of a dark, moonless night to evade the Revenue cutter (whose movements were carefully noted) and to stand in to the rocky coast at a prearranged spot. Here, in some quiet cove, the gang, which usually included one or two farm labourers with a thorough knowledge of the nearby country, would be waiting. With a look-out stationed on the cliff above to give warning of approaching danger, the work of landing the kegs went on as rapidly as the men knew how, and if all went well the kegs were soon safely stowed away in a farm outhouse or cave and the smugglers dispersed. For those not actually sharing in the 'run', a guinea amply repaid a night's work, together, of course, with a sample of the liquor. If, on the other hand, the landing was interrupted, it might well mean a spell in Bodmin gaol – no healthy place in those days.

One such landing is said to have been made at Lantic Bay, close to Polruan, in 1835. According to the story, the *Daniel and William* landed a cargo of tubs one Friday night, and the Revenue cutter *Fox* having sailed down to the westward on the Saturday morning, it was thought safe to fetch the tubs inland that night. Unexpectedly the crew of the *Fox*, together with the coastguards, and the riding officer, Richard Barrett, burst upon them. Apparently the *Fox*, hard driven, had reached Falmouth and with a favourable wind had got back to Fowey by ten o'clock the same night. A scuffle followed, during which some of the smugglers were secured; strangely enough, none of them was convicted when they appeared at Bodmin Assizes.

Bodinnick boatyard: once a favourite landing place for contraband goods, now a popular ferry crossing to Fowey for visitors.

Official records tell of another landing in 1845 at Coombe on the Fowey side of the harbour entrance. The original plan was to run boldly into Fowey harbour and land the goods at Bodinnick, but an informer had been busy and, gaining knowledge of this, the smugglers decided to drop their cargo in Coombe cove. This was the second method in use and enabled the vessel to get quickly away without having to lie too long off the land. It meant, however, that the tubs, sunk in shallow water with an unobtrusive buoy attached, later had to be located and dragged up. Their first plan having gone astray, it is said that the Bodinnick ferry boat was taken from her moorings and used to bring up or 'creep' the cargo. However, the Polruan Coastguard got wind of the affair and were soon pulling away in their galley to the spot. One of their number, named Piper, patrolling the coast, had meanwhile walked right into the hands of the smugglers waiting in the darkness of night for their companions to bring the boat in to the beach, and he was immediately seized and tied down to a rock, but not before he had managed to fire off one of his pistols. With the arrival of the Polruan coastguards, the smugglers fled. The haul must have been a pretty big one, for over £200 was distributed as prize money in September 1845.

Falmouth harbour in the eighteenth century.

Falmouth

The Falmouth postal packet ships were heavily implicated in smuggling. The packet crews ran what amounted to a mail order service in contraband goods on such a scale that the authorities were eventually compelled to crack down.

In November 1815, a packet ship named the *Duke of Marlborough* was seized by Customs officers who found tea, spirits, pepper and other prohibited goods on board when the ship returned from Lisbon. All members of the crew, apart from the captain and the surgeon, were dismissed. A little over four years later, 3 gallons of rum, 4¾ gallons of geneva, 4 lbs of tea and salt and oranges were found concealed on board. The ship was again seized and the captain fined £20.

A different form of smuggling was attempted in December 1821. The ship's storekeeper, Robert Weens, showing remarkable enterprise, thought it would be profitable to sell gunpowder in Lisbon to local insurgents, so he concealed eight 25 lb barrels of gunpowder on board at Falmouth. They were found before the ship sailed and he was discharged. Problems continued, however. In 1822 the *Duke of Marlborough*'s boat was seized by the Customs tide surveyor in Falmouth after finding '5 quarts of Rum, 4 lbs Pepper, ½lb Tea and 24 lbs of Figs' aboard her.

Above: Falmouth Custom House.

Right: Custom House steps, Penzance.

Newlyn harbour.

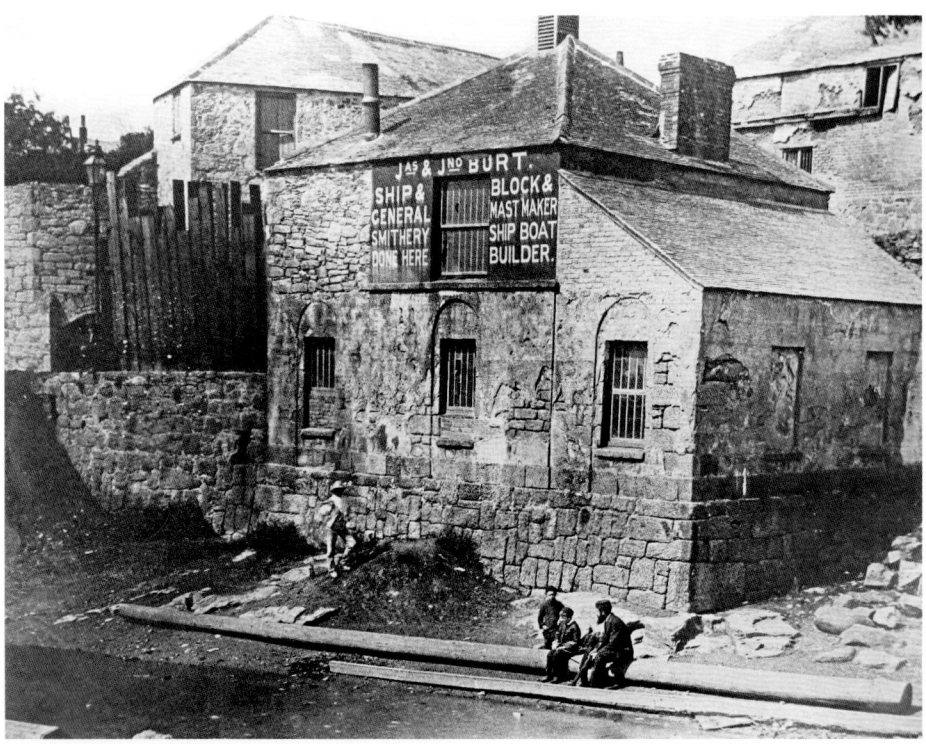

Burt's shipbuilding works at the bottom of Jennings Lane, Penzance.

Penzance and Mount's Bay

Many Mount's Bay fishermen were active smugglers. The seasonal fisheries, accompanied as they then were with fairly long slack periods during the winter, left them with time on their hands and the winter months with their long dark nights also favoured smuggling. Despite the increased risk from storms, the better odds of avoiding detection by the Revenue cruisers seem to have been a deciding factor, coupled with the build-up towards the festive season of Christmas and the New Year, when the spirit market was most buoyant.

One of the earlier accounts of Mount's Bay fishermen being directly involved in smuggling relates to the seizure of a Mousehole shallop by HMS *Wolf* at the end of 1771. Having seized the shallop, the *Wolf*'s commander, Captain William Williams, seems to have misappropriated her to his own use. Ignoring the niceties of legal condemnation, he employed her as an unofficial tender to increase smuggler arrests – mainly because the sailing qualities of the *Wolf* were so poor he had little chance of overhauling any smugglers in a sea chase.

Of course it was not just Newlyn and Mousehole fishermen who were involved in smuggling. The whole of the south coast of Cornwall was a hotbed of smuggling, with occasional pockets on the north coast. In economic terms, fishing craft tended to be one step removed from mainstream maritime trades. Fishing itself was generally a subsistence living rather than an industry. Apart from the Cornish seine fishery, fishing attracted little capital investment. The main ports of Falmouth, Fowey, Looe, Padstow, Penryn, Penzance, St Ives and Truro were all designated as Custom House out-ports, as was Gweek, a village at the head of a tidal river serving the nearby inland town of Helston and its hinterland. The official port limits for most of these out-ports extended some way along the coast on either side, and it was here, away from the main port activity that fishing was mainly centred. By the very nature of these places, quiet creeks and backwater havens, the secretive business of smuggling could take hold and flourish.

One very successful Helston attorney, Christopher Wallis, regularly looked after the affairs of local smugglers and privateers. In some respects his activities mirrored those of Zephaniah Job, who acted on behalf of the smugglers in Polperro – the singular difference being that Wallis was a qualified lawyer. Even so, he was once prosecuted for a smuggling-related offence, and he too acted as the local agent for many of the Guernsey merchants who supplied the smugglers.

He took up professional duties at Helston in 1764, and in later years admitted having regularly kept a journal. He lived well, if unostentatiously, and as a member of the Helston gentry he frequently dined with local Customs officers, magistrates, merchants and bankers while regularly buying wine and spirits from the smugglers. Throughout, Wallis regularly represented the Carters of Prussia Cove, although his journals reveal little of the nature of their smuggling business. Christopher Wallis was particularly successful in securing the restoration of smuggling craft to their owners; in one period during 1800/01 he had more than six such cases current.

As often as not, the local gentry, including even magistrates, financed smuggling enterprises. In 1750, the Mayor of Penzance was bound over 'not to be again guilty of smuggling'. The reckless daring of the smugglers was undoubtedly due to the protection they tacitly received from those in authority. In 1750, for instance, the excise officer at Penzance seized a cargo from a vessel lying off in the bay. The magistrates, however, promptly dismissed the case and the collector of Customs was forced to ask for protection in case he himself should be served with a writ by the smugglers! On another occasion an excise officer, in the process of taking charge of contraband goods discovered at a house in Marazion, had a silver spoon slipped into his pocket. The smugglers subsequently charged him with stealing this, and he was forced to appear at the next assizes.

The gravestone of Thomas James, aged thirty-five, who was killed by a Customs officer in December 1814 while sailing from St Ives round to Flushing.

IN A FRENCH PRISON.

An artist's impression of Harry Carter of Prussia Cove.

West Briton & Cornwall Advertiser
19 February 1830

The men on the preventive service at St. Just near Land's End, aided by a party from the *Dove* revenue cutter, last week seized 173 tubs of spirits and 20 tubs of tobacco which had been landed from a cutter and hidden in a shaft of a mine at that place. During the search, one of the preventive men named White fell from a plank into a shaft of the mine and was killed on the spot. The deceased was a native of St. Just and led the party to the place where the seizure was effected.

Prussia Cove, fortified by the Carters to keep the Revenue officers at bay.

Cornwall's coastline conceals many a cave.

The Carters of Prussia Cove

Among the more notorious of the Cornish smugglers are the Carters of Prussia Cove in Mount's Bay. From their haven they held sway over the smuggling trade from 1770 to 1807. Of this celebrated gang, brothers John and Harry Carter emerge as the principal characters with John as the self-styled 'King of Prussia' and the name subsequently given to his 'kingdom', Prussia Cove.

The Carter family had all the necessary credentials for exploiting the smuggling trade that thrived in Cornwall at the end of the eighteenth century. Their home, Prussia Cove (originally Port Leah), was difficult to reach from the landward side, at least without being seen, but it offered convenient slipways for landing cargoes of contraband goods. The Carter brothers were fine seamen, owners of two large vessels: a 19-gun cutter of 160 tons, and a 20-gun lugger, each with a crew of around thirty men and equipped with at least one smaller boat for close inshore work.

Harry Carter's autobiography tells of running battles with Revenue vessels amid smoke-billowing cannons and the splintering of masts. In one such battle in 1788, he describes how 'the bone of my nose was cut right in two and two very large cuts in my head that two or three pieces of my skull worked out afterwards.' Though grievously hurt, Harry fled from the scene and remained in hiding for three months while his wounds healed.

While Harry ran the transport side of the business, John concerned himself with sales and distribution, an occupation also not entirely free from violence. On one occasion, from a gun battery high on top of the cliffs, John and his followers poured cannon fire into a Revenue cutter that was attempting to follow one of the Carters' vessels into Prussia Cove. Later the cutter returned fire and, when Customs officers joined in the attack from the landward side, John and his men had to seek refuge in a friendly house nearby.

Despite these bloody encounters, at other times an uneasy truce appears to have existed between the Carters and the Customs authorities. Poorly paid and disliked by many of the people among whom they lived, minor officials were unwilling to put their lives at risk, while others were more than happy to turn a blind eye in return for a bribe. Besides, John Carter's honest character was held in high regard; even the excise men recognised his fair dealing.

On another occasion, when the authorities had seized contraband from Prussia Cove, storing it in the Customs House at Penzance, John broke in and took back his 'property', while leaving other goods untouched. 'John Carter has been here,' reported one of the Customs officers. 'We know it because he has taken nothing away that was not his own.'

In 1803, the Carters' property in Prussia Cove was offered for sale by auction, although some said this had been arranged to convince the authorities that the family were now 'going straight'. At the time a copper mine was opened on the cliffs overlooking the cove, and on the slipways where brandy barrels had once been hauled ashore, now coal was landed to drive the mine's newly installed steam engine. Perhaps the new-found wealth from mining proved more lucrative than smuggling, but we do know that the reign of the King of Prussia came to a close around 1807. Shortly after this John's name disappears from the scene, while Harry is known to have retired to a farm nearby, living out his final years preaching in the neighbourhood. Other members of the Carter family are said to have continued the family business into the 1820s, but the success of the improved Revenue service in seizing contraband became ever-more effective. And in 1825, the building of a coastguard station at Prussia Cove put an end, once and for all, to the King of Prussia's smuggling realm.

Smugglers House.

Cadgwith Cove, once a favourite landing place for contraband.

Next page above: Cape Cornwall.

Next page below: Scilly Isles map.

SCILLY ISLES

ON THE SAME SCALE AS THE MAP

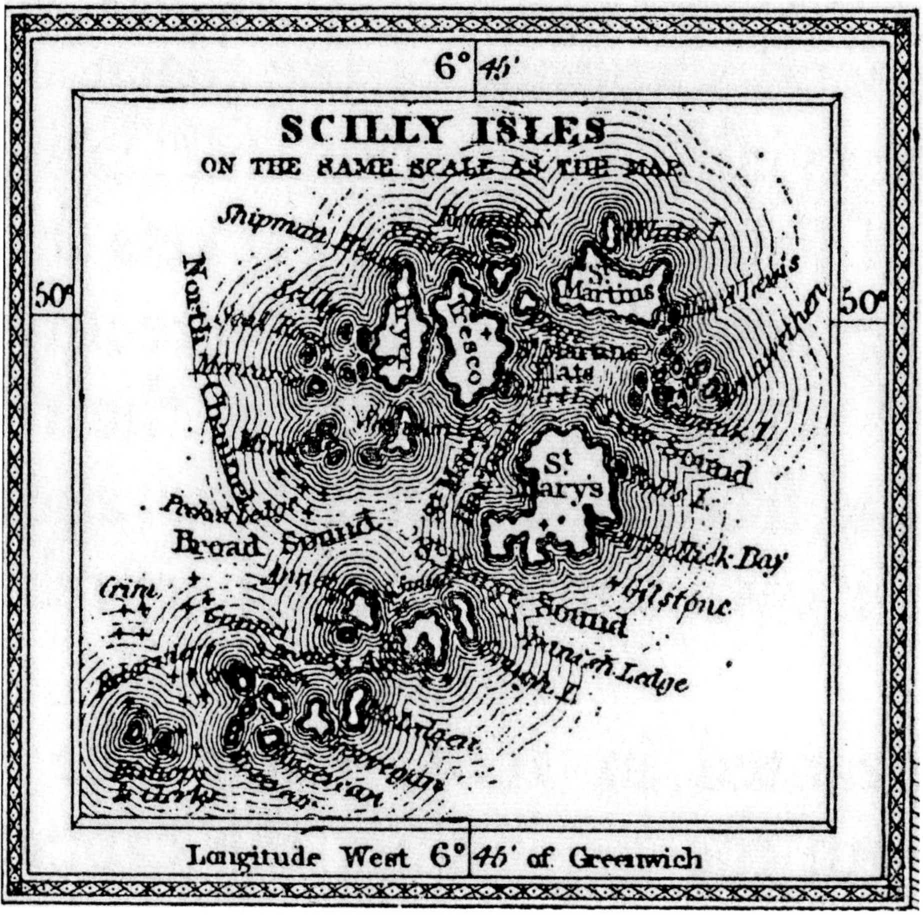

Longitude West 6° 45' of Greenwich

Scilly Isles

The Scilly Islands were once used extensively as a base for contraband goods imported from France and the Channel Islands, most of which was carried onwards to other locations around the coast of Cornwall. Smuggling was therefore the mainstay of the islands' economy, and the Scillies were for a long time a valuable staging post for smuggling in the West Country.

This came to an end with the establishment of a preventive boat on the islands in the early part of the nineteenth century. By 1828, a force of twenty-three officers and men was distributed between the islands of St Mary's, St Agnes, St Martin's and Tresco. Smuggling, however, continued for many years thereafter. In January 1831, the coastguard commander there reported:

> Foreign spirits, tea and tobacco may be had in any quantities at two or three days notice, but not without despatching a vessel to France, which illegal traffic the vessels and boats are at all times ready to engage in that belong to these islands, as they are a complete nest of smugglers.

St Mary's harbour, Scilly Isles, once the centre of a flourishing trade in contraband.

Sunset over Tresco, Scilly Isles.

The Smugglers Den Inn at Cubert, near Newquay, Cornwall. (Photo by Martin Norman, the Inn Sign Society)

North Cornwall

The north Cornwall coast was less frequented by smugglers than the south, largely because of the rugged and forbidding nature of the coast itself, one of the most notorious in the British Isles for wrecks. Much of it was, and still is, remote.

A few miles north-east of Boscastle, at the southern end of Widemouth Bay, lies Millook Haven, where the fishermen took advantage of its isolated position to engage in smuggling on the side.

West Briton & Cornwall Advertiser
5 January 1821

Whereas it has been represented to the Commissioners of His Majesty's Customs that on the night of Saturday, 11th, Sampson Woodcock, chief boatman, and his men were out on duty in the preventative boat stationed at Boscastle in the county of Cornwall for the prevention of smuggling, and went on shore at a place call Millook Haven and seized from four to five hundred tubs of foreign rum spirits, and hauled their boat on to the beach and remained to guard their seizure; that soon after a smuggling cutter came into sight and afterwards two armed boats were sent from her, the crews of which, together with the crew of the cutter, commenced firing on the beach, which the preventative men returned until their ammunition was expended; that the smugglers then came on shore and attacked the said Sampson Woodcock and his men, and by superiority of numbers overpowered them, and compelled them to retreat, and after having driven them from the seizure, the said smugglers carried off the six-oared galley belonging to the preventative station and her materials, together with the tubs which the officers had seized and went off to sea.

The said Commissioners, in order to bring the offenders to justice, are hereby pleased to offer a reward of £200 to any person or persons who shall discover and apprehend, or cause to be discovered and apprehended, any one or more of the said offenders, to be paid by the Collector of His Majesty's Customs at the port of Padstow, upon conviction.

NB The said smuggling cutter had sixteen black ports, eight of a side, bulwarks painted with the broad yellow side and a narrow black streak above, red counter with a yellow moulding, dark gaff topsail, dark fore-sail, white job and running bowsprit, and had a topsail yard across.

West Briton & Cornwall Advertiser
2 April 1830

On Monday morning, 48 tubs of brandy and 16 tubs of gin were lodged in the St. Ives custom house stores by the coast guard stationed at Portreath. The spirits were captured the preceding night together with a boat. It appears the boat came from a small sloop rigged vessel which was seen on Sunday hovering off the coast and the persons on board were in the act of landing the cargo within Hell Bay, about 3 miles west of Portreath, and which is bounded by terrific cliffs, termed Hell's Mouth. Mr Mortly, the officer of the Portreath preventive guard, with three of his men, descended these cliffs at the imminent hazard of their lives as a single false step would have precipitated them down the precipice which is about 50 fathoms in height, and at the foot of it they came upon the smugglers, when the boat, her cargo and two of the crew were secured. It appears the smugglers had resolved on making a desperate resistance, as two of the preventive guard who had been at Hayle and were proceeding to join Mr Mortly and his party were encountered near the summit of the cliffs by eight smugglers, who were armed. Shots were exchanged and the preventive men overpowered, one of them named Rice having received a ball in the thigh. Rice lies ill at Gwithian, to which place he was carried, and is under the care of Mr Angove, surgeon of Hayle, by whom the ball has been extracted.

Gooden Heave cover, Portreath.

It wasn't only smuggling vessels that got into difficulties in the often treacherous waters around the coast of Cornwall. The coastguard service was also on hand to save life whenever a ship was wrecked, as well as protect any cargo that might be salvaged.

Cruel Coppinger

Smuggling in Cornwall has long been the subject of legend and tales handed down from one generation to the next. The story of 'Cruel Coppinger' may well be one such, told by the vicar of Morwenstow, the Reverend Robert Hawker. According to him, Coppinger came ashore at Marshland Mouth, a remote spot on the north Cornwall coast, the sole survivor of a shipwreck, and rode off on horseback with the local heiress whom he later married. He then embarked on a ruthless career as head of a notorious gang, wrecking, stealing and smuggling.

There was indeed a man named Daniel Coppinger who was wrecked at nearby Welcome Mouth just over the county border in Devon in December 1792. When he married a local girl the following year his occupation was given as 'of the King's Royal Navy'; little else is known of him except that he became bankrupt in 1802 and spent time in gaol.

Rev. Robert Hawker.

Left: Cornish caves were a favourite hiding place for smuggled goods.

Below: Custom House quay, Falmouth, in the days of sail.

Jack Rattenbury

Jack Rattenbury is another character who features in the tales of West Country smugglers. He is remarkable because, like Harry Carter of Prussia Cove, he wrote an account of his life: *Memoirs of a Smuggler* was published in 1837. Rattenbury was in fact from Beer in south Devon, but his smuggling escapades to Alderney led to his capture in the Channel by the *Alarm*, a Revenue vessel that took him to Falmouth, where he stood trial and was committed to Bodmin gaol. On the way, he escaped from his escort during a stop at an inn named Indian Queens and fled across the moors to Newquay, where he was given shelter by some local smugglers who led him to Mevagissey the next day where he boarded a boat and returned to Devon.

From an old Print.

JACK RATTENBURY.

Jack Rattenbury.

The Coastguard Service

For most of the latter part of the eighteenth century and throughout the wars with France, the smuggling community in Cornwall had enjoyed something of a holiday. Efforts to prevent the illicit running of cargoes had existed for many years, largely carried out by the Revenue cutters that patrolled the Channel coast, commanded by naval officers. But in 1816, at the end of the war, the land branch of the Customs and Excise, run by Customs officers, was briefly amalgamated with the sea force to form a 'coast blockade' until 1822 when it was renamed the coastguard under the control of the Board of Customs.

The newly formed service consisted of riding officers, a military force on land; the preventive water guard looking after ports and harbours (one of the first such units had been located in Polperro in 1801); the Revenue cruisers at sea, and a small local force known as the coast blockade. Gradually a network of coastguard stations located at strategic points around the coast of Cornwall developed, some of which still survive today.

Henry Shore, who lived at Fowey and held a senior position in the coastguard service there in the 1870s, quotes from intelligence reports supplied by correspondents in Roscoff and elsewhere.

In November 1824, a correspondent at Roscoff not only named six well-known smuggling vessels in port there, but also gave their probable destinations. Two of them were Polperro craft, the *Cruzier*, expected to run her cargo at St Austell Bay (she landed her last crop at Mevagissey), and the *Exchange*, probable destination at St Austell Bay, near the Blackhead. In June 1826, Shore tells us, because several well-known smuggling vessels were absent from Cawsand and thought to be taking in cargoes at Roscoff, the Revenue cutter *Harpy* of the Plymouth station was sent across to find out what she could. She discovered five vessels, of which one was the *Hope* of Polperro. A note accompanying the report said 'these boats being outside of their limits are liable to seizure on attempting to return to the English coast.'

It was a tough world, whether on the side of the Revenue or against it. Shore reports an incident in February 1827 when the commander of the Revenue cruiser *Lion* was reprimanded for allowing his boat's crew to take by force part of a 'seizure' made by the boats of the Looe and Polperro stations. The *Lion* men, anxious to share in the seizure, tried to carry off some of the tubs 'crept' up by the Polperro boat's crew under command of the chief officer of the station. The men from the cruiser were so reckless with their knives in cutting off the tubs from the sinking rope that several of the chief officer's fingers were severely cut.

Shore lists a few smuggling seizures in 1833:

August. One hundred and fifteen tubs belonging to the *Dove* were taken by the Looe coastguard.

September. Five tubs washed ashore near Looe, and a boat marked *Fox*, of Plymouth, found on the beach a mile west,and another tub in the cliff close by. Fifty-seven tubs belonging to the *Elizabeth* are crept up by the Looe boat off Seaton.

October. Fifty-eight tubs out of sixty, forming the cargo of the *Dove*, are crept up off Downderry by the Looe boat.

Near Constantine in November 1828 there was a violent confrontation between a large party of smugglers (armed with pistols, bludgeons and knives) and two Customs officers, in which one of the latter was beaten extensively and left for dead. At nearby Gweek in September 1840, a band of smugglers, angry that their contraband had been confiscated, forced their way into the Helford Custom House and recovered the loot.

Violence was not the only danger that the officers faced. On the north coast of Cornwall, beyond the River Camel, the Preventive men operating from Boscastle and Bude had an especially lonely and inhospitable stretch of cliffs to patrol. In January 1822 the Boscastle preventive men were returning from a foray from Bude when the wind and sea got up and the boat was upturned off St Gennys. Locals observing the tragedy from the cliff tops were powerless to help, and all five men were drowned.

Port Quinn.

Talland Bay as it was 100 years ago, and ...

... as it is today, the scene of a drug smuggling arrest in 1979.

Twentieth Century

On 17 September 1979, Customs and Excise and police seized a converted fishing boat in Talland Bay, just east of Polperro, and brought to an end what was thought then to be Britain's biggest drugs smuggling gang.

Over a period of four years the motor yacht *Guiding Lights* had undertaken twenty-two voyages from the Mediterranean and had shipped 30 tons of very good quality Moroccan Gold cannabis with a street value of £30 million from Gibralter.

Initially this illicit cargo was landed in the Torbay area, but then the gang bought Rotterdam Cottage in Talland Bay. Roderick Eagleton, who lived in the cottage and ran the Talland Bay café, admitted his part in the smuggling and was jailed for three years. At the Old Bailey twelve men were jailed for a total of fifty-five years and fined over £675,000. The last to be brought to justice was Ronald Taylor in 1986 – he had jumped bail in 1981 – and he was jailed for six and a half years and fined £234,750.

When the authorities swooped on Rotterdam Cottage and Talland café, 1.5 tons of cannabis valued at £2 million was found in a specially built secret underground store behind the café's counter. After the discovery of keys at Taylor's Middlesex home, and the licence for *Guiding Lights*, over 2 tons of cannabis was found in a garage in Penge, South London, as well as £250,000 in cash. The main trial lasted two months in 1981 and the mastermind behind the gang, London bookmaker Robert Mills, was jailed for ten years.

Perhaps this episode shows that some things have not changed as much as one might have thought in Cornwall's smuggling history ...

Lugger at sunset.

Further Reading

Arnold-Foster, D., *At War With The Smugglers* (1936).

Barton, R. M. and D. Bradford Barton, *Life In Cornwall* (extracts from the *West Briton*) (1970).

Beck, John, *Captain John Bull of the Falmouth Packet Service* (SWMHS Maritime Monograph) (1995).

Couch, Jonathan, *The History of Polperro* (1871).

Doe, Helen, *The Maritime History of Cornwall* (2006).

Halliday, F. E., *A History of Cornwall* (1959).

Hamilton Jenkin, A. K., *Cornwall and its People* (1970).

Harper, C., *The Smugglers* (1909).

Hippisley Coxe, Antony, *Smuggling in the West Country 1700–1850* (1984).

Jamieson, A. G. (ed), *A People Of The Sea* (1986).

Johns, Jeremy Rowett, *The Smugglers' Banker* (Polperro: Polperro Heritage Press, 1997).

Keast, John, *The Story of Fowey* (1950).

Noall, Cyril and D. Bradford Barton, *Smuggling In Cornwall* (1971).

Phillipson, David, *Smuggling 1700–1970* (1973).

Pickering, Isabel, *Some Goings On* (1995).

Platt, Richard, *Smuggling In The British Isles* (2011).

Pollard, J., *The Autobiography of a Cornish Smuggler (Captain Harry Carter)* (1900).

Stephens, W. B., *The Seventeenth Century Customs Service Surveyed: William Culliford's Investigation of the Western Ports 1682–84* (2013).

Waugh, Mary, *Smuggling in Devon & Cornwall 1700–1850* (1991).

Webb, William, *Coastguard: An Official History of HM Coastguard* (1976).

The Cornish Magazine, Vol. 1 (1898) and Vol. 2 (1899).